T0328649

Cambridge Elements

Elements in Development Economics
Series Editor-in-Chief
Kunal Sen
UNU-WIDER and University of Manchester

HIERARCHY OF NEEDS AND THE MEASUREMENT OF POVERTY AND STANDARDS OF LIVING

Joseph Deutsch
Bar-Ilan University and Ashkelon Academic College

Jacques Silber
Bar-Ilan University

CAMBRIDGE
UNIVERSITY PRESS

Shaftesbury Road, Cambridge CB2 8EA, United Kingdom

One Liberty Plaza, 20th Floor, New York, NY 10006, USA

477 Williamstown Road, Port Melbourne, VIC 3207, Australia

314–321, 3rd Floor, Plot 3, Splendor Forum, Jasola District Centre, New Delhi – 110025, India

103 Penang Road, #05–06/07, Visioncrest Commercial, Singapore 238467

Cambridge University Press is part of Cambridge University Press & Assessment, a department of the University of Cambridge.

We share the University's mission to contribute to society through the pursuit of education, learning and research at the highest international levels of excellence.

www.cambridge.org
Information on this title: www.cambridge.org/9781009485975

DOI: 10.1017/9781009358200

© UNU-WIDER 2024

First published 2024

A catalogue record for this publication is available from the British Library.

ISBN 978-1-009-48597-5 Hardback
ISBN 978-1-009-35817-0 Paperback
ISSN 2755-1601 (online)
ISSN 2755-1598 (print)

Additional resources for this publication at www.cambridge.org/deutsch-silber

Hierarchy of Needs and the Measurement of Poverty and Standards of Living

Elements in Development Economics

DOI: 10.1017/9781009358200
First published online: February 2024

Joseph Deutsch
Bar-Ilan University and Ashkelon Academic College

Jacques Silber
Bar-Ilan University

Author for correspondence: Jacques Silber, jsilber_2000@yahoo.com

Abstract: The focus of this Element is on the idea that choice is hierarchical so that there exists an order of acquisition of durable goods and assets as real incomes increase. Two main approaches to deriving such an order are presented, the so-called Paroush approach and Item Response Theory. An empirical illustration follows, based on the 2019 Eurobarometer Survey. The Element ends with two sections showing, first, how measures of inequality, poverty, and welfare may be derived from such an order of acquisition and, second, that there is also an order of curtailment of expenditures when individuals face financial difficulties. This title is also available as Open Access on Cambridge Core.

Keywords: consumption expenditures, durable goods, Eurobarometer, hierarchical choice, inequality, Item Response Theory, order of acquisition, order of curtailment, Paroush approach, poverty, welfare

ISBNs: 9781009485975 (HB), 9781009358170 (PB), 9781009358200 (OC)
ISSNs: 2755-1601 (online), 2755-1598 (print)

Contents

An online Appendix for this publication can be accessed
at www.cambridge.org/deutsch-silber

1 Introduction

For most economists an important assumption underlying the notion of rational behavior is that economic agents compare bundles of goods by reducing everything to a common denominator, called utility. For example, standard consumer theory assumes that the loss of some units of a given commodity in one bundle can be compensated by the gain of some units of another commodity. Some economists have, however, questioned such an assumption and adopted the notion of hierarchical preferences. As stressed by Drakopoulos (2004), although the concept of hierarchical preferences leads to a reasonable system of choice, most economists rejected such an approach because they focused their attention on the notion of lexicographic ordering, which, as is well-known, violates the axiom of continuity and, thus, in the eyes of these economists, cannot have a wide application when applied to economic issues. They cite here an argument emphasized by Debreu (1959), according to which lexicographic orderings produce nonconvexities and discontinuities, and these shortcomings tend to prevent the existence of a general equilibrium.

Pasinetti is one of those rare economists who argued in favor of hierarchical preferences as he wrote: "Although possibilities of substitution among commodities are of course relevant at any given level of real income, there exists a hierarchy of needs. More precisely, there exists a very definite order of priority in consumers' wants, and therefore among groups of goods and services, which manifests itself as real incomes increase" (Pasinetti, 1981, p. 7, cited by Lavoie, 1994).

Lavoie (1994), in fact, argues that most economists put too much emphasis on substitution effects and tend to neglect income effects. He cites the famous textbook of Deaton and Muellbauer (1980, p. 71), who concluded that, when working with general categories of consumption expenditures, own-price and cross-elasticities are very small (not higher than 0.5 in absolute value for the own-price elasticities of categories such as, for example, food, travel, and entertainment). The explanation Lavoie provides for such findings is that these large categories of expenditures are derived from needs that cannot be substituted. Therefore, variations in the price index of these large categories will not lead to important changes in consumption patterns. One can expect, however, that substitution effects may be more substantial within each of these consumption categories, although some empirical findings of Houthakker and Taylor (1970) seem to indicate that even in such a case price-elasticities are not very high.

This emphasis on groups of goods appeared already in the 1940s in an important article of the French economist René Roy (1943), who wrote that it is possible "to establish among all the goods and services, a classification into groups such that any consumer has access to a group of a certain order only after having ensured the satiety of the needs responding to the groups of lower category."[1] The novelty of Roy's approach is that, looking at necessities, he divides the consumers of these goods into two groups: whereas the first one did not reach satiety, the second one did. He then derives the law of demand as a function of the distribution of incomes, as will be shown in Section 2.

In Section 2 we discuss the notion of hierarchical choice as it appeared in the economics literature. Special emphasis is put on the contribution of Roy who is well known for what is called Roy's identity (Roy, 1947) which enables one to derive the ordinary demand curve (not the compensated one) once we know the indirect utility function. However, Roy, according to Allais (1988), made another important contribution, which Schultz (1938) considered as fundamental, namely his analysis of the relationship between the laws of demand and Pareto's (1895) law of income distribution.

In section 3 we apply this notion of hierarchical choice to the idea of an order of acquisition of durable goods and assets. This notion was originally introduced by Paroush (1965), following previous work by Guttman (1944). This section will therefore describe the methodology suggested by Paroush. It will then present an alternative approach to deriving the order of acquisition of durable goods, namely Item Response Theory. The latter approach, though originally appearing in the psychometric literature, turns out to be also relevant to find the most common order of acquisition of durable goods or assets. The section ends with a summary of the so-called Borda approach and of a count approach derived from the structure of the ownership of durables or assets.

Section 4 is devoted to empirical applications. Using the 2019 Eurobarometer Survey we first apply the approach of Paroush to this data base and derive the most common order of acquisition of durable goods for each of the thirty-five countries for which data were available. We then do a similar analysis using Item Response Theory and examine to what extent the orders of acquisition obtained with each approach are similar. We also check whether the rank

---

[1] Our translation. Born in Paris on May 21, 1894, René Roy was admitted to the École Polytechnique in 1914. On August 15 of the same year he had to join the army and he was seriously injured on April 14, 1917, during the attack on the Chemin des Dames: he completely lost his sight. He was only twenty-three ... However, thanks to his strong will he finally managed to calmly accept the unacceptable and to pursue, for sixty years, a career as an engineer as well as economist ... .René Roy's ability to analyze very difficult questions and to keep constantly up to date with the main publications of his time was quite admirable in view of his blindness. René Roy has shown what unyielding energy combined with remarkable intelligence can give, in the face of irremediable adversity (translated by us from Allais, 1988)

correlation between the orders of acquisition observed in two countries is related to the gap in their per capita GDP.

In Section 5 we derive measures of inequality, poverty and welfare from the information obtained on the order of acquisition of durable good and assets in each country. We first give a theoretical background which explains how it is possible to measure inequality, poverty, and welfare when only ordinal variables are available, which is the case of the data we analyze. Then we present empirical illustrations that allow us to estimate for each country, using the orders of acquisition derived in the previous section, the extent of inequality, poverty, and welfare.

Finally in Section 6 we apply the approach of Paroush and Item Response Theory to another type of dataset, namely the Social Survey that was conducted in Israel in 2013. This is the most recent Israeli social survey where respondents were asked whether they had to curtail their expenditures because of financial difficulties, and if they did, which expenditures they reduced or eliminated. In other words, the focus of this section is on the order of curtailment of expenditures, and it should be clear that with this type of information it is also possible to apply the approach of Paroush or Item Response Theory.

Concluding comments are finally given in Section 7.

2 Economics and Hierarchical Choice

We consider it essential to link the phenomena of consumption and consequently of demand to the concept of hierarchy of needs. (Roy, 1943)

2.1 Introduction

The notion of a hierarchy of needs or wants is an old one. Plato in his famous Republic already wrote[2] that "the first and the greatest of our needs is the provision of food to support existence and life ... The second the provision of a dwelling place, and the third of clothing ... ." Much later on, as stressed by Drakopoulos (2004), several economists such as Smith, Say, Jevons, Menger, and Marshall, were also aware of the importance of making a distinction between basic and nonbasic needs. Some of them even proposed a system of choice based on this idea. However, the fact that incorporating hierarchy into the formalistic methodology of the marginalists was not an easy task, explains probably why such a hierarchical approach to decision making, did not become very popular.

---

[2] This citation appears in Drakopoulos (2004).

The goal of this section is to take a closer look at this notion of hierarchy of needs and at its implications. After briefly reviewing the way some famous economists understood the idea of hierarchy of needs, we look at the notion of wants which for some economists is derived from that of needs while others do not really make a distinction between these two notions. Particular attention is then given to the writings of the quite famous French economist René Roy whose articles on the concept of hierarchy of needs are unfortunately not very well known because they were published in French. For Roy the notion of hierarchy of needs applies to broadly defined categories of goods while substitution between goods take place within each of these categories when relative prices change. The last sections (Sections 2.6, 2.7, and 2.8) are devoted to the implications of the concept of hierarchical choice for the shape of Engel curves, the distribution of wealth and poverty and the diversity of expenditures.

2.2 The Notion of Needs

The notion of need has existed for a long time. Smith, for example, explains in the *Wealth of Nations* (pp. 869–70) what he means by "necessaries":

> By necessaries I understand, not only the commodities which are indispens-
> ably necessary for the support of life, but whatever the custom of the country
> renders it indecent for creditable people, even of the lowest order, to be
> without. A linen shirt, for example, is, strictly speaking, not a necessary of
> life. The Greeks and Romans lived, I suppose, very comfortably, though they
> had no linen. But in the present times, through the greater part of Europe,
> a creditable day-labourer would be ashamed to appear in publick[3] without
> a linen shirt, the want of which would be supposed to denote that disgraceful
> degree of poverty, which, it is presumed, nobody can well fall into without
> extreme bad conduct. Custom, in the same manner, has rendered leather shoes
> a necessary of life in England. The poorest creditable person of either sex
> would be ashamed to appear in publick without them.

Almost one hundred years later, as mentioned by Becchio (2014), in the first edition of his *Principles of Economics* (1871, 1981), Carl Menger stressed the fact that there are four prerequisites for a good to be an economic good: "the presence of a human need; some properties able to render a thing capable of being brought into a causal connection with the satisfaction of this need; the human knowledge of this causal connection; a command of the thing sufficient to direct it to the satisfaction of the need" (Becchio, 2014). Menger's views imply first that the existence of a human need is only a necessary condition but not a sufficient one for a thing to become a good. As stressed by Ruprecht

---

[3] The spelling "publick" is the one which appears in the original work of Adam Smith and this is why we kept this spelling and did not write "public."

(2007) this suggests that the existence of an objective cause–effect relationship is a necessary condition for a thing to become a good. In addition, an individual consumer must be aware of this relationship. Ruprecht gives as illustration the discovery of the impact of citrus fruits on scurvy prevention. Citrus fruits had been known for a long time for their caloric content, their juiciness, their taste, but the connection with the prevention of scurvy was something new of which people became aware only around the middle of the seventeenth century. Clearly the objective impact of citrus fruit consumption on the prevention of scurvy does not imply that consumers are aware of this effect. Ruprecht, however, challenges Menger's (1953) view, according to which the objective character of this relationship is a necessary condition for a thing to become a good. He cites Hayek (1979), for whom subjective beliefs matter if we want to explain human behavior toward things. For Hayek what is relevant is not what can be found about things by the objective methods of science, but what a person thinks about them. "Knowledge, which we may happen to possess about the true nature of the material thing, but which the people whose action we want to explain do not possess," is not relevant to explain the actions of individuals. Ruprecht then asks how people should take a decision when consumers face competing cause–effect hypotheses. Following Popper (1959) he argues that "non-falsification" may be a plausible criterion. But what happens when consumers need to choose between several hypotheses that have not yet been falsified but there is no way of testing them? In such a case consumers will have to decide which hypothesis they trust and whether there is a case strong enough for them to act.

As far as the fourth condition mentioned by Menger is concerned ("a command of the thing sufficient to direct it to the satisfaction of the need"), one could have thought that income is a precondition for getting "personal command" of something. But the concept of "positional goods," introduced by Hirsch (1976), shows that consumers acquire wants via their consumption experiences as well as when observing the consumption of other people. Ruprecht mentions then the concept of "emulative consumption" stressed, for example, by Bourdieu (1984), a behavior often summarized by the expression "keeping-up-with-the-Joneses." In short Ruprecht concludes that social imitation provides a strong argument against giving "personal command" the status of a necessary condition for a thing to become a good.

In fact, Becchio (2014) has argued that in the second edition of Menger's *Principles* (1923), Menger's views were somewhat different as he then emphasized the notion of social needs and social goods. As mentioned by Yamamori (2020), the second edition of Menger's *Grundsätze* (1923) had a new first chapter whose title was "theory of needs." In this chapter Menger wrote that "the starting point for any investigation of economic theory is needy human nature. Without needs, there would be no economy, no national economy, no economic science" (Menger, 1923, cited by Yamamori, 2020). Yamamori also stressed that Menger makes a distinction between need ("Bedürfnis" in German) and "its satisfier-provisions" ("Bedarf" in German), which is defined as "the quantities of consumption goods a person must have to satisfy his needs." The former notion is considered as subjective, the second as objective.

At the same time as Carl Menger published the first edition of his Principles, Stanley Jevons (1871) published his *Theory of Political Economy*. Both authors took a subjective approach to the theory of value, at the difference of the objective approach of classical economists. Jevons's analysis is based on the concept of utility, while Menger uses the word "satisfaction." As mentioned by Lagueux (1997), for Jevons, utility is "the abstract quality whereby an object serves our purposes and becomes entitled to rank a commodity" (Jevons, p. 38), while for Menger, satisfaction describes a subjective state of mind. Menger refers "to degrees of satisfaction in relation to various needs which are considered and draws comparisons only between these different degrees of satisfaction" (Lagueux, 1997).

Note that in his essay on "Economic possibilities for our grandchildren," Keynes (1933, pp. 833–41) considered that there are two types of needs: absolute and relative. While absolute needs are satiable, relative needs are not because "they satisfy the desire for superiority" (Keynes, 1933).

2.3 From Needs to Wants

Needs have to be carefully distinguished from wants. As stressed by Lutz and Lux (1979) needs can be hierarchically classified and determine consumers' behavior. Wants are derived from needs and may be substituted for each other. They reflect "the various preferences within a common category or level of need" (Lutz and Lux, 1979).

For Drakopoulos (1994) a need implies something which is universally necessary, while a want refers to a personal preference and the latter is a trait of the individual. This difference explains why there may be an important degree of substitution between wants, while there is likely to be only a weak degree of substitution between needs, which are assumed to be universal. Such a view echoes that of Cosmides and Tooby (1994), who argue that cultural differences are vastly overstated, "because beneath existing surface variability all humans share the same set of preference-generating and decision-making devices." Such a statement is derived from an evolutionary psychology approach to human behavior. For Cosmides and Tooby (1994) "natural selection's invisible hand created the structure of the human mind, and the interaction of these minds is what generates the invisible hand of economics." These authors also stress that evolutionary psychology can provide a list of human universal preferences, and of the "procedures by which additional preferences are acquired or reordered." Such an approach would widen the scope of preferences and not limit the latter to goods and services. Earl and Potts (2004) have thus proposed a distinction between high- and low-level preferences. High-level preferences are innate, while low-level preferences refer to specific preferences that are acquired by learning and specialization. Such a distinction between high- and low-level preferences is a consequence of human's "bounded rationality." Consumers "have a problem of knowing what they want and how to get it" (Earl and Potts, 2004). While high-level preferences define in a way the problems that must be solved, low-level preferences have to be acquired either by learning or via agents that Earl and Potts call "preference entrepreneurs," who are able to adapt products to lifestyles.

Another interesting approach is that of Witt (2001), who asked what wants people pursue in their daily economic activities, wants they satisfy by consuming resources as direct inputs or as tools for serving these wants. Witt's main argument is that there is a biological foundation of certain "basic needs" (e.g. thirst, hunger, sex) and they are fixed and universally shared. Biological evolution requires organisms to consume certain things to survive and this explains why, among the very poor, everyone spends most of his/her money consuming food. Once the basic needs are satisfied, consumers move on to satisfy other needs that may be "learnt." Here Witt makes a distinction between cognitive and noncognitive learning. The latter concerns acquired wants that emerge as consumers "form associations between these experiences and the material environment which surrounds them."[4] Cognitive learning, on the contrary, refers to a kind of problem-solving sequence where consumers try to find new solutions to a given problem.

2.4 On the Notion of Hierarchical Choice

This notion of hierarchy has been stressed by Drakopoulos (1994), who presents a survey of hierarchical choice in economics. He starts by reminding us that this is an old idea since Plato, as indicated at the beginning of this section, had a hierarchical view of needs. Drakopoulos then emphasized the fact that the notion of hierarchical choice appears in a way or another in the works of Jevons

---

[4] Chai (2017) gives here the case of consumers who if "repeatedly exposed to a certain type of bed sheet when they sleep may acquire a liking for such bed sheets that exists independently of how tired they are."

(1871, 1957), Marshall (1949), Menger (1871, 1981) but also Fishburn (1974), Little (1950) and many other economists. Here are some interesting citations. Georgescu-Roegen (1966), for example, wrote:

> It has long since been observed that human needs and wants are hierarchized Satisfactions of concrete needs have different degrees of importance to us . . . Despite the fact that the want pattern differs from one individual to another, most of these patterns have a great deal in common. (1) The hierarchy of wants seems to be for all men identical up to a certain rank. One may be almost sure that this refers at least to thirst, hunger, leisure, shelter. (2) Individuals belonging to the same culture are likely to have in common still a greater number of wants at the top of the hierarchy than those common to all men.

This is the reason why

> choice aims at satisfying the greatest number of wants, starting with the most important and going down their hierarchy. Therefore, choice is determined by the least important want that could be reached . . . . No matter what we choose, houses, cars, or combinations of commodities, the procedure is the same. Between two combinations the choice will be made according to the lowest relevant want that can be reflected in any of the two combinations.

Robinson (1956, p. 354, cited by Lavoie, 1994) argues that, "generally speaking, wants stand in a hierarchy (though with considerable overlaps at each level), and an increment in a family's real income is not devoted to buying a little more of everything at the same level but to stepping down the hierarchy."

For Pasinetti (1981, p. 73, cited by Lavoie, 1994), although possibilities of substitution among commodities are, of course, relevant at any given level of real income, there exists a hierarchy of needs. More precisely, there exists a very definite *order of priority* in consumers' wants, and therefore among groups of goods and services, which manifests itself as real incomes increase."

Eichner (1986, pp.159–60, cited by Lavoie, 1994) believes that "in an economy that is expanding over time, it is the income effect that will predominate over the relative price, or substitution effects . . . Substitution can take place only within fairly narrow subcategories. Consumers' preferences are, in this sense, lexicographically ordered . . . ."

As emphasized by Lavoie (1994), for those economists, like the so-called "post-Keynesian economists," for whom a hierarchy of needs exists, households whose incomes are relatively similar will satisfy their needs in more or less the same order. This is so because of convention. In other words, once physiological needs are fulfilled, there will still be a common hierarchy of needs for individuals who share a similar culture. Consumers tend to conform to the norms of reference groups and they tend to imitate the behavior of those who are higher in the hierarchy of society. This idea that the relative position of consumers in society matters very much is not new, as it was already raised by Duesenberry (1949), Leibenstein (1950) and Veblen (1931).

2.5 Hierarchy of Needs and the Approach of René Roy

The French economist René Roy, famous for introducing what is known as Roy's identity (Roy, 1947), introduced the notion of group of goods and assumed the existence of a hierarchy of goods (Roy, 1930, 1931, 1933, 1943). More precisely he made a distinction between what he calls "inferior and superior groups." In his words[5] (Roy, 1931):

> Under these conditions, everyone will obtain the quantity of goods necessary to satisfy the needs corresponding to the lower groups of the classification, to devote the surplus to the products ranked in the higher groups. Our reasoning is therefore based on the notion of satiety, itself deriving from the principle of decreasing utility. Moreover, we assume that the amount of income spent on meeting the needs of a certain group is the same for every individual, and therefore does not depend on the value of the income. This is a hypothesis which may seem paradoxical, but which is nevertheless justified by the following considerations:
>
> 1) For fairly large incomes, the share allocated to the acquisition of objects belonging to the lower categories of needs represents only a very small fraction of the individual income.
> 2) If we refer to the previously mentioned Pareto formula, we can easily see that the number of people with an income greater than a given value decreases very rapidly when this value increases.

As will be seen, Roy makes a link between the distribution of incomes and the general expression of the law of demand. As far as the allocation of one's income between the various goods is concerned, Roy (1930, p. 115) writes:

> Whatever the importance of the income, there exists, for each individual, a certain order of priority relative to the allocation of his resources to each type of article. This classification in individual needs could be highlighted by a method analogous to that which was used by Dupuit (1844) for the appreciation of the utility of the various goods; it would be enough, assuming that all prices remain constant, to imagine that the income of the individual in question decreases progressively, in such a way that he is obliged to gradually eliminate the articles which he considers the least indispensable.

---

[5] Roy published several articles in *Econometrica*, all of them in French. To the best of our knowledge these articles, at least most of them, have not been translated in English and hence were cited very seldom. This is why we cite him at length in this section. The translation is ours.

For all the people belonging to the community studied, the classification would obviously not be the same for all individuals, because of differences in taste, but one can imagine the possibility of forming groups of items such that, for all individuals, the order of priority is observable, not from one item to another, but from one group to the other . . .

The categories in question would ultimately reflect the hierarchy of needs, while within these categories, the selection of items would be made according to individual tastes; we therefore make a distinction between needs and tastes.

Roy (1930) then derives the following result concerning the price elasticity of the demand for necessities.

Let P and Q refer to a price and quantity index of the goods of a given group and p_i and q_i to the price and quantity of good i which belongs to this group. We may therefore write that

$$PQ = k \sum_i p_i q_i$$

where k is a constant. Let P_0 and Q_0 refer to the value of the price and quantity indices at some original time 0.

Roy then defines as r_0 the lower limit of individual incomes. He also defines (Roy, 1930, pp. 121–2) as q_l "the maximum value of the quantity index for each individual." He then writes:

we have previously admitted that this limit ensuring satiety for the group of products studied was the same for each individual and that it did not depend in particular on the amount of individual income. This limit q_l is such that if the price index corresponding to the group studied is equal to P, the individual income ensuring satiety is represented by the product $q_l P$.

To arrive at the law of demand for basic necessities, we will observe that the set of payments Q.P relating to this category of objects, can be divided into two groups:

a) The group of people whose individual consumption is imperfect and therefore remains below the q_l limit.

b) The group of consumers whose individual income is sufficient to allow the purchase of the quantity limit q_l.

For the first group, that is, for individuals whose income is between the lower limit r_0 and the income Pq_l enabling them to acquire the quantity-limit q_l, the total income is allocated to the acquisition of objects belonging to the group studied, since they are, by hypothesis, objects of first necessity.

The set of payments for this group of goods will hence be expressed as

$$\int_{r_0}^{Pq_l} rn(r)dr$$ where r refers to income and $n(r)$ to the number of individuals

with an income r.

For the second category of individuals, those whose income allows satiety, all the payments corresponding to basic necessities are equal to the
product of individual income Pq_l by the number of people whose income is
higher than this amount; the set of payments in question is therefore represented by the expression $Pq_l \int_{Pq_l}^{\infty} n(r)dr$.

We may therefore write that

$$PQ = \int_{r_0}^{Pq_l} rn(r)dr + Pq_l \int_{Pq_l}^{\infty} n(r)dr.$$

Roy (1930, pp. 127–8) then derives PQ with respect to the price, and this
derivative, using the second member of PQ, is equal to $q_l \int_{Pq_l}^{\infty} n(r)dr = Q_s$
where Q_s refers to the total consumption of those people whose income is
greater than Pq_l, that is, to the total consumption of those who are able to ensure
satiety for the products considered.

Roy (1930) then concludes that

$$d(QP) = PdQ + QdP = Q_sdP$$

$$\leftrightarrow P\frac{dQ}{Q} + \frac{QdP}{Q} = \frac{Q_s}{Q}dP \leftrightarrow \frac{dQ}{Q} + \frac{dP}{P} = \frac{Q_s}{Q}\frac{dP}{P}$$

$$\leftrightarrow \frac{dQ}{Q} = \frac{dP}{P}\left(\frac{Q_s}{Q} - 1\right) \leftrightarrow \frac{dQ}{Q} = -\frac{dP}{P}\left(\frac{Q - Q_s}{Q}\right)$$

$$\leftrightarrow -\frac{\left(\frac{dQ}{Q}\right)}{\left(\frac{dP}{P}\right)} = -\lambda = \left(\frac{Q - Q_s}{Q}\right)$$

$\lambda = \left(\frac{Q - Q_s}{Q}\right)$ may hence be considered as the price elasticity of the "necessities."
It is estimated as the ratio of the consumption of necessities of those who do not
reach satiety over the total consumption of necessities in society. This price
elasticity will hence be lower, the higher the percentage of individuals who
reach satiety, as far as necessities are concerned.

It is interesting to note that Lavoie (1994), referring to the work of Deaton and
Muellbauer (1980), concluded that "those who have attempted to estimate the
importance of pure substitution effects on the general categories of consumption expenditures, after having taken into consideration the income effects
through time, have discovered that these substitution effects, own-price elasticities and cross-elasticities, are quite negligible." Lavoie (1994) added that "the
findings of Houthakker and Taylor (1970) show that even at a much more

disaggregated level, that is, with over eighty categories of consumer goods, consumption expenditures are mainly determined by habits and income effects, while price substitution effects play a fairly modest role."

In another paper Roy (1943) repeated his belief in the notion of hierarchy of needs. Here is what he wrote:

> With regard especially to the phenomena of consumption, we finally think that the notion of urgency in the satisfaction of human needs tends to create a scale of consumer goods which can thus be classified into groups, while the notion of taste manifests itself within each group by fixing the choice of each consumer on the articles corresponding to his personal preferences. Within these groups, the phenomena of complementarity or substitution also appear, which thus contribute to fixing the demands of consumers for the various articles considered separately . . .. (Roy, 1943, p. 14)
>
> We have implicitly assumed that prices are given because, theoretically, the order of succession of goods for a consumer depends on the relative values of prices. But the price variations do not affect, in our view, the general arrangement of the scales, because by triggering substitution phenomena they only move the scales inside each group and only modify their respective positions, without altering the classification of groups. The notion of hierarchy of needs and consequently of commodities is in fact governed by motives of a physiological, moral or psychological order, indifferent to a large extent to the price movements that one observes in practice. (Roy, 1943, p. 16)
>
> Given the assumption made about the allocation of income, any price variation concerning a group of rank i will have no influence on the demand of the groups of lower order, while it will have an impact, not only on the demand for group i but on those of all groups of higher order. We can also express this fact by saying that price variations for luxury items have no influence on the demand for basic necessities or on that of products that simply provide a degree of comfort that cannot be assimilated to luxury. If we want to concretize our thought further, we can still say that variations in the price of champagne wine will not have an influence on the consumption of table wine, but that conversely a variation in the price of table wine may indeed act on the demand for champagne wine . . .
>
> By limiting ourselves to two goods, bread and wine for example, and by admitting that each consumer has free access to all the water he needs, we come to the following conclusion:
>
> 1) Every consumer first allocates his income to the acquisition of bread, until he obtains the satiety of his need for food, and for a homogeneous group of consumers this satiety is obtained for a substantially constant consumption of bread, whoever is the consumer:
> 2) Once satiety has been obtained for the need for food, every consumer allocates the surplus of his income to the acquisition of wine.
> 3) The demand for bread is independent of the price of wine, but the demand for wine depends on the price of bread. (Roy, 1943, p. 20)

The notion of groups rests precisely on the hypothesis that the degree of urgency of the various needs experienced by men is linked to their physiological nature, to their psychological state, to mores, or to the organization of society, in a word, to a whole set of factors independent of the price level. It is only within each group that the respective levels of the various prices, combined with individual tastes, direct the demands towards this or that article, by the mechanism of substitution. (Roy, 1943, p. 22)

2.6 Implications for Engel Curves

Once choice is assumed to be hierarchical, there are, as stressed by Drakopoulos (1994), implications concerning the shape of demand and Engel curves. The notion that for each good there is some satiety level of consumption which is supposed not to be surpassed, whatever the individual's income, has been stressed in several empirical analyses. Prais (1952), for example, suggested that when selecting a mathematical formula for the Engel curve, one should make sure that it has such an asymptotic property. An upper asymptote is certainly desirable for necessities but, as stressed by Aitchison and Brown (1954), it is less obvious for luxury goods. They, however, argue that "many commodities begin life as luxuries and eventually become semi-luxuries or necessities as increasing incomes and falling prices bring consumers nearer to an ultimate saturation level."

In what is considered as the first statistical analysis of budgets, Engel (1857, 1895) proposed the following law of consumption (see Stigler, 1954): "The poorer a family, the greater the proportion of its total expenditure that must be devoted to the provision of food." Wright (1875) gave then what Stigler (1954) labeled an "excessive free translation of Engel's law" since Wright mentioned four propositions:

First, the greater the income, the smaller the relative percentage of outlay on subsistence. Second, the percentage of outlay on clothing is approximately the same, whatever the income. Third, the percentage of outlay for lodging, or rent, and for fuel and light, is invariably the same, whatever the income. Fourth, as the income increases in amount, the percentage of outlay on "sundries" becomes greater.

Stigler (1954) mentions that Schwabe (1868, 1966) added the following law: "The poorer anyone is, the greater the amount relative to his income that he must spend on housing." Wright (1875) also suggested the following generalization (see Stigler, 1954): "The higher the income, generally speaking, the greater the saving, actually and proportionately."

Engel, in fact, seems to have borrowed a notion introduced by Smith and according to which "the ultimate measure of welfare is the degree to which individuals are able to satisfy what Engel called "Bedürdfnisse" and which Chai and Moneta (2010) translated as "wants." More precisely Engel (1895, p. 1) wrote that "every individual directs (out of his own impulse) his highest interest to the continuous satisfaction of those wants that stem directly from his human nature, to the expansion of these wants, and also to the attainment of the necessary means to satisfy the higher, expanded wants." As stressed by Chai and Moneta (2010), Engel "shifted the focus of research away from examining how expenditure is distributed across individual goods consumed, towards focusing on how it is distributed across wants which goods ultimately satisfy. Second, Engel made a clear break from the common tendency amongst classical economists to assume that some "basic" goods are inherently more important to human welfare than other 'luxury' goods."

This emphasis on wants appears clearly in his empirical work since he did not really focus his attention on food expenditure but on "nourishment" which also included expenditure on alcohol and tobacco. According to Chai and Moneta (2010), Engel believed that his empirical analysis showed that there was a hierarchy among wants, the most important want being the want for nourishment. Then there was the want for clothing, accommodation, heating, and lighting. Engel also stressed that when a family is not able to satisfy all its wants, it is likely to decide not to satisfy "higher-order" wants so that it can satisfy its basic wants.

The most famous approach to the idea that there exists a hierarchy of needs is certainly that of Maslow (1970). The first set of need that he identifies is that of basic needs, which include air, water, food, sleep, and sex. The second group of needs refers to safety needs, like feeling safe and secure and settled. These are more psychological than physiological needs. The third set of needs is "belonging needs," which concern the desire to belong to families, clubs, etc. As stressed by Clarke (2005) "this level of needs incorporates the need to feel (nonsexual) love and acceptance of others." The fourth level of needs covers self-esteem needs, that is, the need to be admired by those around you. The last level of needs is labeled "self-actualization," summarized by Clarke (2005) as the "self-fulfillment of ones' own potential," although one may wonder whether such a want is universally shared.[6]

A few papers have attempted to test this notion of hierarchy of needs. Thus Hagerty (1999) adopted Maslow's notion of hierarchy of needs as well as his classification into five categories of needs: physiological, safety, belonging and love, esteem, and self-actualization. The indicators he used for physiological needs were the number of daily calories available per person and then GDP per capita. For safety needs he used safety from war, safety from murder, and high

---

[6] We thank Andreas Chai for having drawn our attention to this point.

life expectancy. For belonging and love the indicators were low divorce rate and low child death rate. For esteem the measures were political rights and women's participation in work for pay. Finally for self-actualization the indicators used were tertiary, secondary, and primary education enrollment.[7] Data were available for eighty-eight countries between 1960 and 1994. Hagerty (1999) tested four hypotheses to confirm Maslow's theory. First, that nations increasingly fill their needs over time. Second, a nation's trajectory of need fulfillment follows an S-shaped pattern. Third, nations' sequence of need fulfillment follows Maslow's sequence. Fourth, higher growth in one need area is correlated with lower growth in other need areas. The results indicated that the three first hypotheses were generally confirmed, but not the fourth one.

Jackson and Marks (1999) adopted Max-Neef's (1989, 1991) characterization of human needs and applied it to an analysis of the patterns of consumer expenditure in the United Kingdom between 1954 and 1994. Both Maslow (1970) and Max-Neef (1991) characterize certain needs as material needs. Material needs are mainly subsistence and protection needs. More generally, satisfying these needs requires materials. Non-material needs are more about processes (personal, social, and cultural) than about objects. Thus "participation, affection, understanding, idleness, creation and freedom relate more to individual and social psychology than they do to material things" (Jackson and Marks, 1999). In their empirical analysis, Jackson and Marks observed that the increase between 1954 and 1994 in expenditures related to material needs satisfaction was 50 percent, while the increase related to non-material needs satisfaction was 160 percent. But this increase in nonmaterial needs appears to be dominated by expenditure on material goods (increase in goods and durable goods rather than in services) and therefore remains a material-intensive form of consumption.

Clarke (2005) adopted Maslow's classification of needs, which makes a distinction between basic needs (*BN*), safety needs (*SN*), belonging needs (*BIN*), self-esteem needs (*SEN*), and self-actualization needs (*SA*), to estimate well-being. He assumed that well-being *WB* could be considered as self-actualization *SA* and expressed it as the following function:

$$WB = SA(BN, SN, BIN, SEN)$$

BN was assumed to include two indicators: daily calories available per person and access to safe water. For *SN* the indicators were infant mortality and life expectancy, for *BIN* they were telephone mainlines and fertility rates, and for

---

[7] This link between education and self-actualization is probably oversimplified, as there certainly is a complex map between spending and wants. We again thank Andreas Chai for having stressed this point.

SEN the indicators were adult illiteracy and unemployment. Clarke gave a higher weight to higher needs and decided to give to BN, SN, BIN, SEN the weights 1, 2, 3, and 4, respectively. Clarke also used normalized indexes by dividing each year's figure by the highest figure occurring throughout the time series he used.

Chai and Moneta (2012) attempted to test Engel's approach to a hierarchy of needs. Engel had made a distinction between the following needs ("Bedürfnisse"): nourishment, clothing, housing, heating and lighting, tools for work, intellectual education, public safety, health and recreation, and personal service. Chai and Moneta used the UK Family expenditure surveys for the years 1961, 1970, 1980, 1990, and 2000 and allocated the various household expenditure data to the need categories classified by Engel and mentioned previously. They then observed that between 1960 and 1980 the expenditure shares of these various needs for the lowest-income decile did not vary very much. After 1980, expenditure on nourishment declined significantly while housing expenditure increased significantly. They concluded that their results were quite consistent with Engel's observed patterns. In particular, the budget shares of household expenditure on needs that Engel considered as central to physical sustenance dominate low-income consumption patterns in all years examined. These authors also observed that Engel curves for lower-order goods have shapes that are more similar to each other than to the shapes of Engel curves for higher-order goods, while Engel curves for higher-order goods have shapes more similar to each other than to shapes of Engel curves for lower-order goods. Chai and Moneta concluded that "a hierarchy of needs appears to consist of two levels in that it is only the most important needs, the need for nourishment, that appears to dominate over other needs. There appears to exist no order between other lower order needs."

2.7 Implications Concerning the Distribution of Wealth and Poverty

These implications have been analyzed in a very interesting way by the French engineer and economist Dupuit (1859). Here is what he wrote:[8]

If, when the insufficiency of the harvest is a tenth, everyone reduced their consumption by a tenth, there would doubtless be deprivation; however [. . .] the suffering would nowhere be very acute; but this is not the way of things: however expensive bread may be, it is still, for the rich and well-to-do classes, the most economical food, and for them the high price of bread is never a reason to consume less. The rich or well-to-do household that spent 400 francs on bread

---

[8] The paragraphs below are a translation of the citations of Dupuit given in Simonin (2009).

will spend eight if the price doubles, but the expenditure on other items in its budget is reduced by 400 francs [. . .].

If half the population consumes, in times of scarcity, the same quantity of bread as in times of plenty, then all the deprivation must fall on the other half. It is then no longer a question of a tenth but of a fifth, and [. . .] such a reduction in food [. . .] is distributed in a very unequal way among the lower classes, according to the resources at their disposal, and afterwards this deprivation of bread entails many others; because, to satisfy this imperious need of hunger [. . .] the poor man sells his clothes, his blankets, his mattresses, deprives himself of wood, of light, and thus suffering from hunger, cold and humidity, falls prey to disease, and finds only in death the end of his sufferings [. . .]. Others [. . .] by dint of privations on secondary needs, can wait for better times. Finally, in the well-to-do classes, not only is there no deprivation, but there is an increase in consumption. For, by the very fact that the lower classes have been obliged to restrict their consumption relative to certain objects, these objects, the production of which has not diminished, are offered to the rich classes at a lower price

Let us not lose sight of the fact that in this phenomenon of the distribution of wealth, we must always arrive at the result that consumption is equal to production. Now we suppose that there is no decrease in production except on the article of cereals, and it is a fact [. . .] that in times of scarcity the poor classes are obliged to renounce any other expense than that of their food; it is therefore necessary that in these circumstances the other classes consume what the poor classes have not been able to consume. [. . .] which compensates for the excess expenditure which they have to do to get bread.

We will say: first, that scarcity is borne entirely by the poor classes of society, and even in a very unequal way between them; second, that for the poorest the deprivation of food is complicated by a host of other deprivations, [. . .]; third that these privations are the only ones suffered by the slightly higher classes; fourth, that the wealthy classes, far from supporting it of any kind, can consume more. (Dupuit [1859], p. 163–4 3)

Chai and Moneta (2012) also analyzed the implications of a hierarchy of needs on the diversity of expenditures. They thus noted that households located at low- or medium-income deciles tend to diversify their consumption patterns.

2.8 Implications Concerning the Diversity of Expenditures

Somewhat similar conclusions were derived by Chai et al. (2015). Using data from the 2001 cross-section of the UK Household Expenditure Survey and gathering information on the expenditures of over 5000 households over twelve different categories, they measured diversity over different expenditure levels, using various diversity measures. They concluded that, at low-income levels, households have relatively concentrated spending patterns but tend to diversify their spending quickly as their income rises. At the same time, the level of heterogeneity in spending diversity also grows with income.

Chai et al. (2022) started from the idea that at very low-income levels household demand is mainly dedicated to food, while richer households consume a much wider variety of goods, higher-quality goods, and more services. Economic growth, however, is often accompanied by rising income inequality. Therefore, if one assumes hierarchical preferences, greater income inequality will raise the distance between consumers across the spending hierarchy and hence lower the homogeneity of consumption patterns. Another reason why the homogeneity of spending patterns is likely to decline as household incomes rise is that relatively affluent consumers may concentrate on niche luxuries that may be specific to each consumer (see Neiman and Vavra, 2019). Chai et al. (2022) based their empirical analysis on the World Bank's Global Consumption Database (GCD), which provides 2011 data covering ninety countries, mainly from the less developed countries. The GCD covers 107 expenditure categories: 32 are food and beverages, 41 are services, and 34 are goods. These 107 expenditure categories are also aggregated into 10 larger groups: food, clothing, health, electricity, passenger transport, housing, means of communication, education, recreation, personal transport. Interestingly the GCD also provides data on the percentage of households in each income segment who consume a particular good. These segments are uniform across countries and are based on the global distribution of per capita income. The lowest-income segment corresponds to the bottom half of the global distribution; the low-income segment to the 51th to 75th percentiles; the middle-income segment to the 76th to 90th percentiles, and the high-income segment to the 91st percentile and above.

As mentioned previously, the focus of the Chai et al. (2022) paper was on diversity. They concluded their empirical investigation by stressing that among low levels of per capita GDP, spending diversity grows via a diversification of the food diet of the consumers, while at higher levels of per capita GDP, spending diversification takes place via an increase in the range of services that are consumed. Chai et al. (2022) then argue that these observations tend to support the thesis that the rise in the service sector may well be the consequence of shifts in final demand related to the growth of the per capita GDP. They also concluded that higher income inequality tends to reduce the average share of households consuming a particular good and that, in more affluent countries, there was a negative correlation between the level of income inequality in a country and the number of varieties consumed. Among poor countries, however, it appears that income inequality has a positive impact on the number of varieties consumed, confirming previous findings by Falkinger and

Zweimuller (1996). Chai et al. (2022) also found that expenditure hierarchies observed in the world have a common characteristic, namely that the income elasticity of food is always lower than that of other goods and services. However, among higher-order goods, expenditure hierarchies are more country-specific. As far as niche consumption is concerned, it appears that the diversification of consumption among poor consumers is quite homogenous, while rich people tend to concentrate spending into different areas so that there is a decrease in the homogeneity of demand.

In a recent paper on the International Comparison Program (ICP), purchasing power parity (PPP), and household expenditure patterns, Clements et al. (2022) initially concluded that in all the surveys they analyzed there is enough evidence confirming Engel's law. But they also stressed that Engel's law has implications concerning the structure of relative prices: given that the income elasticity of food is smaller than one, one can expect a decline in the relative price of food as income grows. Using the 2011 ICP data, Clements et al. also found a confirmation of an empirical regularity observed by Working (1943): the proportion of total expenditure devoted to food tends to decrease in arithmetic progression as total expenditure increases in geometric progression. An additional implication may be derived from what Clements et al. called "Working's law," namely that food will attract a smaller fraction of an increment of income among the rich than among the poor.

2.9 Concluding Comments

This section attempted to show that the concept of hierarchical choice is not a new one, as it appears implicitly or explicitly in the writings of famous economists. It was also shown that this notion has far-reaching implications, not only concerning the shape of Engel curves and the diversity of expenditures but also pertaining to the distribution of wealth and poverty. The focus of the next two sections will be on one of the implications of the notion of hierarchical choice, namely the idea that there is an order of acquisition of durable goods. Two ways of deriving such an order will be presented: Section 3 will first focus on the approach of Jacob Paroush (1963, 1965, p. 973) which is related to the notion of Guttman (194) scale; then it will present what is known as Item Response Theory.

3 Deriving the Order of Acquisition of Durable Goods and Assets: Methodologies

3.1 Introduction

While the focus of Section 2 was on the notion of hierarchical choice in the history of economic thought, this section looks at one aspect of hierarchical choice, namely the idea that there is an order of acquisition of durable goods and assets. We will show that there are two main approaches to the derivation of such an order. One is inspired by Guttman's (1944) work on the scaling of qualitative data and led Paroush (1963) to assume that there is an order of acquisition of durable goods and to propose an approach allowing one to discover such an order. The other approach is borrowed from the field of psychometrics and applies the technique known as Item Response Theory to the derivation of such an order of acquisition of durable goods and assets. The section ends with a short presentation of two other ways of looking at the order of acquisition of durable goods and assets, one which applies to this issue the concept of Borda rule and the other one whose emphasis is on the structure of asset ownership.

3.2 On the Guttman (1944) Scale

Assume a qualitative variable (also called "attribute") which includes several categories (e.g. various religions) which do not have any intrinsic ordering. Assume that y is such an attribute, while x is a quantitative variable which we can divide in a certain number of intervals which will have a one-to-one correspondence with the values of y. In such a case we can state that the attribute y is a simple function of x. Guttman gives the example of a variable x which can take ten values (0 to 9) and for which the following correspondence exists:

x	0	1	2	3	4	5	6	7	8	9
Y	y_1	y_1	y_1	y_3	y_3	y_2	y_2	y_2	y_2	y_2

Guttman then states that "for a given population of objects, the multivariate frequency of a universe of attributes will be called a *scale* if it is possible to derive from the distribution a quantitative variable with which to characterize the objects such that each attribute is a simple function of that quantitative variable. Such a quantitative variable is called a scale variable."

Guttman then stresses that one should not expect to observe perfect scales and that the deviation from a perfect scale will be measured via what he calls a *coefficient of reproducibility*. This coefficient gives the relative frequency with which the values of the attributes correspond to the intervals of a quantitative variable. Guttman calls *scale score* a value of a scale variable and *scale order* the ordering of objects according to the numerical order of their scale scores.

He then considers the following illustration. Assume a mathematical test composed of the following three questions:

- If r is the radius of a circle, what is the area of the circle?
- Which values of x satisfy the equation $ax^2 + bx + c = 0$?
- To what is de^x/dx equal?

The answer given to each question will be either right or wrong. Although a priori there could be eight (i.e. 2^3) patterns of answers given by the different individuals, one may expect that if the individuals are somewhat familiar with this kind of questions, only four types of answers would be observed. For example, a first category of individuals would give a correct answer to all three questions, a second category to the first two questions, a third category to the first question only, and a last category would have given a wrong answer to each of the three questions. If this is the case, the four type of individuals previously described would be respectively given the scores 3, 2, 1, 0. In other words, once we know the score of an individual, we also know to which question he/she gave a correct answer.

Guttman gives then a graphical illustration of this example. Assume, for example, that 80 percent of the individuals gave the correct answer to the first question, 40 percent to the second, and 10 percent to the third. The chart below summarizes these results:

Third question	90%		10%
Second question	60%	40%	
First question	20%	80%	

Guttman (1944) then writes that the multivariate distribution for the three questions, given that they form a scale for the population, may be summarized on the same chart, since all those belonging to the group answering a more difficult question right belong also to the group who gave a correct answer to an easier question. Here is therefore the chart summarizing the results:

20%	40%	30%	10%
Score 0	Score 1	Score 2	Score 3

More generally the Guttman scale includes a list of statements that can be ranked from the least to the most important statement. This implies that if an individual agrees with the last statement on the list, he/she would have agreed with all the previous statements on the list.

The Guttman scale approach has been applied to various types of data, among which data allowing to discover the order of acquisition of assets, mainly of durable goods.

3.3 The Paroush Approach to Discovering the Order of Acquisition of Durable Goods

Sixty years ago, Paroush (1963) proposed to use information which is available on the order of acquisition of durable goods to derive estimates of the standard of living of households.[9] As a simple illustration, assume we have information on the ownership of three durable goods, a refrigerator, a television, and a car. An individual or a household[10] can own one, two, three, or none of these durable goods. It is easy to derive that there are $2^3 = 8$ possible profiles of ownership of these three durable goods. Table 1 shows all the possible combinations of ownership of durable goods. A number 1 implies that the household owns the corresponding good, a zero that it does not.

Let us start by assuming that every household follows the following order: refrigerator, television, car. In other words we assume that the first durable good a household will acquire is a refrigerator. Then if this household desires to acquire a second durable good, it will buy a television. Obviously the third durable good the household will acquire, in our simple illustration, is a car. Note that if this is the order of acquisition of durable goods, there will be no household with the profiles 3, 4, 6, and 7 in Table 1. Profile 3, for example, assumes that a given household acquires only one durable good and that it is a television. But a refrigerator, and not a television, is supposed to be the first durable good acquired by a household.

We do not want to assume, however, that every household will buy first a refrigerator, then a television, and finally a car. There are clearly other possible sequences of acquisition. Moreover, even if we find out what the most common order of acquisition of durable goods is, there are always households that will deviate from this most common order of acquisition. This is why Paroush (1963, 1965, 1973) recommended computing the number of changes in numbers (from 0 to 1 or from 1 to 0), which will put a deviating household back to one of the profiles corresponding to a given order of acquisition of durable goods.

More generally, let us suppose that there are G durable goods. Then, for a given order of acquisition, as we have just seen in the simple illustration of Table 1, there will clearly be only $(G + 1)$ possible profiles in the acquisition path. However, with G durable goods, there will be 2^G possible acquisition profiles, as shown in Table 1 with three durable goods. Call P_j one of the ownership profiles that is allowed, under the order of acquisition of durables that has been selected. More precisely express P_j as $P_j = \{p_{j1}, \ldots, p_{jg}, \ldots, p_{jG}\}$ where each

---

[9] See also Paroush (1965; 1973).

[10] We will hitherto mention only households but the same type of analysis may be conducted if data are available at the individual level.

Table 1 List of possible ownership status when there are three durable goods

Ownership Profile	The household owns a refrigerator	The household owns a television	The household owns a car
1	0	0	0
2	1	0	0
3	0	1	0
4	0	0	1
5	1	1	0
6	0	1	1
7	1	0	1
8	1	1	1

element p_{jg} is equal to 0 or 1 (as in Table 1). Now let Y_i be the vector defining the order of acquisition of household i with $Y_i = \{y_{i1}, \ldots, y_{ig}, \ldots, y_{iG}\}$. We can now compare this acquisition profile Y_i of household i, with each of the $(G+1)$ acquisition profiles P_j that are allowed, for the order of acquisition selected. Let D_i be the smallest distance between the vector Y_i and any of these $(G+1)$ acquisition profiles P_j. In other words we write that

$$D_i = Min_{\text{for the } (G+1) \text{ allowed profiles}} \{|y_{i1} - p_{j1}|, \ldots, |y_{ig} - p_{jg}|, \ldots, |y_{iG} - p_{jG}|\}$$

(1)

Assume now that there are N_i households with the same acquisition profile as household i. Paroush (1963, 1965, 1973) recommended computing what Guttman (1944) called the coefficient R of Reproducibility, which is defined as

$$R = 1 - \left[\frac{\left(\sum_i N_i D_i\right)}{\left(\sum_i N_i G\right)}\right]$$

(2)

since G is the highest possible distance D_i (D_i would be equal to G if, for example, all the elements of vector Y_i are equal to 1 while all the elements of the vector P_j are equal to 0).

Paroush (1963, 1965, 1973) indicated that one can prove that $(\frac{1}{2}) \leq R \leq 1$. Paroush also wrote that "for most practical applications of the order of acquisition of durable goods a population is considered sufficiently 'scalable' if about ninety percent of its purchases are 'reproducible', provided the number of commodities is not very small."

As a simple illustration, let us go back to Table 1 and suppose that the acquisition profile of individual i is profile 4, while the most common order of acquisition of durables is assumed to be as follows: a refrigerator, a television, a car. In such a case only profiles 1, 2, 5, and 8 in Table 1 are possible. We will now compute the distance of the acquisition profile of individual i to each of these four profiles 1, 2, 5, and 8.

The "distance" D_i for an individual with profile 4 to profile 1 in Table 1 will then be expressed as $|0-0| + |0-0| + |1-0| = 1$.

The "distance" D_i for an individual with profile 4 to profile 2 in Table 1 will then be expressed as $|0-1| + |0-0| + |1-0| = 2$.

The "distance" D_i for an individual with profile 4 to profile 5 in Table 1 will then be expressed as $|0-1| + |0-1| + |1-0| = 3$.

Finally, the "distance" D_i for an individual with profile 4 to profile 8 in Table 1 will then be expressed as $|0-1| + |0-1| + |1-1| = 2$.

The smallest distance of the ownership profile of individual i to the possible ownership profiles when the order of acquisition is a refrigerator, a television, a car is therefore equal to 1.

We can proceed similarly for every other individual. We may also define a "standardized distance" D_{si} by dividing the observed distance D_i by its maximal value G. If there are N households in the whole population ($N = \sum_i N_i$), the "average standardized distance" $\overline{D}_{si}$ in the population will be expressed as the weighted average of the "standardized distance" for the various households, that is as

$$\overline{D}_{si} = \sum_i \left(\frac{N_i}{N}\right)\left(\frac{D_i}{G}\right) \tag{3}$$

so that the "proximity index" R turns out to be equal to the complement to 1 of $\overline{D}_{si}$:

$$R = 1 - \overline{D}_{si} \tag{4}$$

Note, however, that we do not know what the most commonly order of acquisition of durable goods in the population is. To find out what it is, we need to compute the distances D_i and the proximity index R for each possible order of acquisition of durable goods. It is easy to check that there are $G!$ such possible orders. Let D_i^h, $\overline{D}_{si}^h$, and R^h be respectively the distance D_i for individual i, the corresponding "average standardized distance" $\overline{D}_{si}$ in the population and the proximity index R when profile h is the one with which the profile of household is compared. The most common order of acquisition in the population will then be the one with the highest value of the proximity index R^h.

Table 2 Possible acquisition profiles with two goods

Acquisition profile	Durable good a	Durable good b
1	0	0
2	1	0
3	0	1
4	1	1

Clearly detecting this most common order of acquisition of durable goods requires a very high number of computations. Assume, for example, that the data give information on ten durable goods. For each household in the survey under study, the determination of the minimum distance D_i for this household will be based on eleven comparisons. Suppose that the survey under study includes 2,000 households. Then $(11 \times 2,000) = 20,000$ comparisons will be needed in order to determine the proximity index for a single order of acquisition. This procedure will have to be repeated $10! = 3,628,800$ times. This is the total number of possible orders of acquisition resulting with ten durable goods. Therefore, $20,000 \times 3,628,800 = 72576000000$ will be the total number of computations necessary to find the order of acquisition with the highest index of proximity R. Given the power of contemporary laptops, having to implement such a high number of computations is not any more a problem.

Here is a simple illustration of the procedure that has just been described. To simplify we will assume that there are only two durable goods, a and b. There are hence four possible acquisition profiles, as shown in Table 2.

We will now assume that there are three individuals named x, y, and z. Table 3 indicates which durable good(s) each of these three individuals owns.

We can now compute the distance between the ownership profile of each of these three individuals and each potential ownership profile. Let us call $d(i;j)$ such a distance where $i = x, y,$ or z and $j = 1, 2, 3,$ or 4. It is then easy to find out that

$$d(x; 1) = 1, \ d(x; 2) = 2, \ d(x; 3) = 0, \ d(x; 4) = 1$$

$$d(y; 1) = 1, \ d(y; 2) = 0, \ d(y; 3) = 2, \ d(y; 4) = 1$$

$$d(z; 1) = 1, \ d(z; 2) = 2, \ d(z; 3) = 0, \ d(z; 4) = 1$$

Table 3 Ownership of durable goods by the three individuals

Individual	Owns good a	Owns good b
x	0	1
y	1	0
z	0	1

Note that these distances are computed by comparing what is in the cell $(i;j)$ in Table 3 with what is in the cell $(k;j)$ in Table 2 where $k = 1, 2, 3,$ or 4 . We then take the absolute value of the difference in each comparison.

The average distance $\overline{d(x, y, z; 1)}$ to profile 1 is then expressed as

$$\overline{d(=x,y,z;1)} = \left(\tfrac{1}{3}\right)[d(x;1) + d(y;1) + d(z;1)] = \tfrac{1+1+1}{3} = 1$$

We can then similarly compute the other average distances and get

$$\overline{d(=x,y,z;2)} = \left(\tfrac{1}{3}\right)[d(x;2) + d(y;2) + d(z;2)] = \tfrac{2+0+2}{3} = \tfrac{4}{3}.$$

$$\overline{d(=x,y,z;3)} = \left(\tfrac{1}{3}\right)[d(x;3) + d(y;3) + d(z;3)] = \tfrac{0+2+0}{3} = \tfrac{2}{3}.$$

$$\overline{d(=x,y,z;4)} = \left(\tfrac{1}{3}\right)[d(x;4) + d(y;4) + d(z;4)] = \tfrac{1+1+1}{3} = 1.$$

We now will look at the two possible orders of acquisition. The first one implies that individuals first acquire good a, and then good b. The second one assumes that individuals first acquire good b, and then good a. In the first case, Table 2 indicates that only profiles 1, 2, and 4 are relevant. In the second case Table 2 not 3 shows that only profiles 1, 3, and 4 are possible.

Let us now examine the first case. We indicate here again the values of the distances $d(i;j)$ where $j =$ only 1, 2, or 4., We then have $d(x;1) = 1,$ $d(x;2) = 2,$ $d(x;4) = 1$ so that the minimal distance for individual x is *Min* $d(x) = 1$. Similarly, $d(y;1) = 1,$ $d(y;2) = 0,$ $d(y;4) = 1$ so that the minimal distance for individual y is 0 and we write: *Min* $d(y) = 0$.

Finally $d(z;1) = 1,$ $d(z;2) = 2,$ $d(z;4) = 1$ so that the minimal distance for individual z is 1 and we write: *Min* $d(z) = 1$.

The average minimal distance of the individuals to the order (a, b) is hence:

$$\left(\frac{1}{3}\right)\{Min\ d(x) + Min\ d(y) + Min\ d(z)\} = \frac{1 + 0 + 1}{3} = \frac{2}{3}$$

We now use the same procedure for the order (b, a). The authorized profiles are here 1, 3, and 4. We then derive that

$d(x; 1) = 1$, $d(x; 3) = 0$, $d(x; 4) = 1$ so that the minimal distance for individual x is 0 and we write $Min\ d(x) = 0$.

Similarly, $d(y; 1) = 1$, $d(y; 3) = 2$, $d(y; 4) = 1$ so that the minimal distance for individual y is 1 and we write: $Min\ d(y) = 1$.

Finally $d(z; 1) = 1$, $d(z; 3) = 0$, $d(z; 4) = 1$ so that the minimal distance for individual z is 0 and we write: $Min\ d(z) = 0$.

The average minimal distance of the individuals to the order (b, a) is hence:

$$\left(\frac{1}{3}\right) \{Min\ d(x) + Min\ d(y) + Min\ d(z)\} = \frac{0 + 1 + 0}{3} = \frac{1}{3}$$

We therefore conclude that on average the three individuals are closer to the order of acquisition (b, a) than to the order (a, b).

3.4 Item Response Theory

Item Response Theory (*IRT*) is a technique that was originally introduced to help educational and psychological assessments.[11] More precisely it was used to analyze the results of psychometric tests, the idea being that the probability of giving a correct answer to a question in the test was a function of the intelligence or ability of the examinee. However, intelligence (or ability) is not a characteristic of the individual that can be easily measured. It is, in fact, a latent trait. To measure it one relies on the answers given to a certain number of questions (items). If the answer to a given question is correct, the individual will receive a score of 1; if it is no correct, his/her score will be 0. Let A refer to the ability of an individual. Given the ability of the individual, the latter will have a probability $P(A)$ to give a correct answer to the item so that individuals with a low ability will have a small probability to give a correct answer, while those with high ability will have a high probability to correctly answer the item. It is assumed that the link between the probability $P(A)$ and the ability A can be represented by a *S*-shaped curve. Such a curve carries the name of "item characteristic curve." For estimation purpose the item characteristic curve will be represented by the Logistic Function (see Figure 1):

$$P(A) = \frac{1}{1 + e^{-A}} \tag{5}$$

While Item Response Theory has been mainly applied in psychology and in the field of education, it has been also used to analyze deprivation and poverty, more precisely multidimensional poverty. The general idea is that poverty has many facets and, like ability, cannot be really measured. Let now R (for richness) refer

---

[11] A good and clear introduction to Item Response Theory is given in Baker (2001).

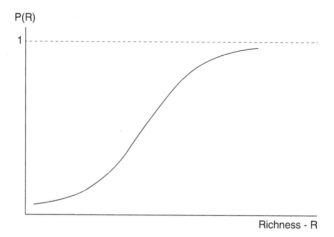

Figure 1 A typical Item Characteristic Curve

to the antonym of poverty. Like poverty, richness will be assumed to be multidimensional. It will not refer only to material wealth. It may also include other positive aspects of life such as good health or good relations with the family. In other words, richness is a latent variable that can be indirectly measured via the answers given to various questions focusing on diverse aspects of wealth in the large sense of this word. Let now $P(R)$ be the probability that, for example, an individual owns a given durable good (item), such as a refrigerator or a car. If the individual owns a car, the individual will have a score of 1 for this item; if he/she does not own a car, his/her score will be 0. Similar assumptions will be made concerning the ownership of other durable goods (items) or the answers given to questions covering other aspects of richness such as those mentioned previously.

Here also it will be assumed that the link between $P(R)$ and R will be represented by a Logistic Item Characteristic Curve that is similar to that given in Figure 1.

Two aspects describe such a curve. The first one, which in the educational literature is called the "difficulty" or "severity" of the item, focuses on the probability that the individual owns the durable good and is determined by the location of the curve. It indicates in fact along the richness scale (represented by the horizontal axis) the probability of owning a good. Therefore, for durable goods that are commonly found among poor individuals, at the left side of the horizontal axis, the characteristic curve will display a relative high probability $P(R)$, and for durable goods that are usually found only among relatively rich individuals, the characteristic curve will display at the same horizontal location a relative low probability $P(R)$.

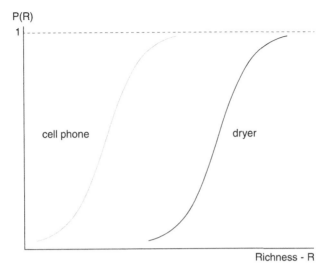

Figure 2 Tow typical Item Characteristic Curves

The second aspect of the characteristic curve is called "discrimination" and focuses on the steepness of the curve. The steeper the curve, the better the durable good (item) under study discriminates between the probability of those who have and those who do not have the good.

Figure 2 displays the Item Characteristic Curve for two different goods. The first one, which refers to a cell phone, has a lower level of difficulty as the probability of owning a cell phone is higher as compared to that of owning a dryer (the second durable good) at all levels of richness R. An extreme case of discrimination would be that of perfect discrimination: those whose richness is smaller than some critical value R_c do not own the durable good, while those whose wealth is above R_c all own the good. Note that in such a case, no distinction is made between those whose richness level is lower than R_c or among those whose richness level is higher than R_c (Figure 3).

The Parameters of the Item Characteristic Curve

The typical shape of an Item Characteristic Curve is that of a logistic curve with two parameters: d (discrimination parameter) and l (location or difficulty parameter). It is expressed as

$$P(R) = \frac{1}{1 + e^{-d(R-l)}} \tag{6}$$

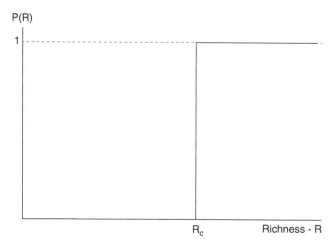

Figure 3 The case of perfect discrimination

The location parameter l is defined as the point on the "richness" axis at which the probability $P(R)$ of having a given durable good is equal to 0.5. In other words, we obtain $P(R) = 0.5$ by substituting in equation (6) $l = R$.

The slope of the Characteristic Curve is given by:

$$\frac{dP}{dR} = \frac{d}{[1 + e^{-d(R-l)}]^2} = d \cdot P(1 - P) \tag{7}$$

Therefore, the larger the discrimination parameter d, the steeper the Characteristic curve.

Estimating the Item Characteristic Curve

The estimation of the Logistic Characteristic Curve is based on the method of maximum likelihood. Each observation is assumed to be a single independent draw from a Bernoulli distribution. In a sample of n individuals for a given good, we define the variable y receiving the value $y_i = 1$ ($i = 1, 2, \ldots, n_1$) with probability P_i for individuals owning the good and the value $y_i = 0$ ($i = n_1 + 1$, $n_1 + 2, \ldots, n$) with probability $1 - P_i$ for individuals who do not have the good.

The join probability or likelihood function is:

$$L = \prod_{i=1}^{n_1} P_i \prod_{i=n_1+1}^{n} (1 - P_i) \tag{8}$$

Taking logs we obtain:

$$\ln L = \sum_{i=1}^{n_1} \ln P_i + \sum_{i=n_1+1}^{n} \ln(1 - P_i) \tag{9}$$

Since $P = \frac{1}{1+e^{-d(R-l)}}$ and $(1-P) = \frac{e^{-d(R-l)}}{1+e^{-d(R-l)}}$ we maximize the log likelihood function with respect to d and l:

$$\max_{d,l} \ln L = -\sum_{i=1}^{n_1} \ln\left[1 + e^{-d(R-l)}\right] - \sum_{i=1}^{n_1} d \cdot (R-l) + \ln\left[1 + e^{-d(R-l)}\right]$$

$$(10)$$

The parameters and their asymptotic variances are derived using the iterative Newton–Raphson method.

The Rasch model: A one parameter model

The Rasch model is based on three assumptions:

- *Uni-dimensionality*: the latent trait is unique, and all the answers given for the different items depend on the same latent trait.
- *Conditional independence of the responses*: for each individual, the answers given to the different questions are statistically independent, given the latent trait. In other words, the latent trait is the only factor that explains the difference between the response patterns provided by two individuals.
- *Monotonicity*: the conditional probability for an individual of not having a car, for example, is a monotonic non decreasing function of the individual level of material deprivation.

Note that within the Rasch measurement approach the items in the scale have similar power in discriminating among respondents; that is, there is equal discrimination of the items. This characteristic differentiates the Rasch model from any other *IRT* model. This characteristic of equal discrimination is also known as parameter separability. In fact in the Rasch[12] (1960) model it is assumed that the discrimination parameter d is equal to 1, whatever the item (e.g. durable good) under study. In such a case expression (6) will be written as

$$P(R) = \frac{1}{1 + e^{-1(R-l)}} \tag{11}$$

It is important to stress that the Rasch model is a confirmatory model. In other words, only when the data meet the Rasch model's requirements can a satisfactory measurement tool be derived. It is therefore of utmost importance to check that the data fit the assumptions of the Rasch model.

---

[12] An expanded edition of his 1960 study, with foreword and afterword by B. D. Wright, was published in 1980 by the University of Chicago Press.

Three Parameters Model

In the psychometric tests literature such a model takes into consideration the fact that individuals may select an answer by just guessing. A third parameter, g, is therefore introduced which is not a function of the ability of the individual. In our case such a parameter would simply indicate the lowest value of the probability of having a durable good and would correspond to the intercept of the item characteristic curve with the vertical axis.

The equation for such a model is then expressed as

$$P(R) = g + (1-g)\left[\frac{1}{1 + e^{-d(R-l)}}\right] \tag{12}$$

The location parameter is now defined as the point on the horizontal axis where the probability $P(R)$ is equal to $(1+g)/2$ and not any more to 0.5. Note that the discrimination parameter d is still proportional to the slope of the item characteristic curve at the point where $R = l$.

3.5 The Borda Approach

In an original paper Fine (1983) suggested deriving the order of acquisition of consumer durables from the Borda Rule which is named after the eighteenth-century French mathematician and naval engineer Jean-Charles de Borda. Borda seems to have devised this rule in 1770, but, according to Brian (2008), 1784 is the correct date of attribution. What is Borda's rule? According to Borda's method, voters are asked to rank the candidates in order of preference from the first to the last choice. The lowest ranking candidate is then given 1 point, the second lowest 2 points, etc., and the top candidate is attributed a number of points which is equal to the number of candidates. Then one adds the number of points given by all the voters to each candidate and the candidate who received the highest number of votes is the winner.

Fine (1983) started by stressing the parallelism that exists between the idea of an order of acquisition of durables and social choice theory. More precisely, individuals are assumed to have an order of priority in acquiring durable goods, and what we are looking for is to find an ordering that would represent the individual orderings in a consistent way. And this is clearly similar to what is done in social choice theory, where individuals are faced with social alternatives, and we are looking for a social ordering that would represent the individual orderings according to some well-defined criteria. The idea is to construct a "representative consumer" who is supposed to represent the preferences of society, but this "representative consumer" does not represent the average in terms of aggregate demand.

Assume n individuals with individual orderings OR_1, OR_2, ..., OR_n.
Here is the set of assumptions made by Fine (1983):

- Symmetry: This is a standard assumption. It says that if we swap the alternative orders as well as the individuals, we will end up with the original order of preference of the "representative consumer."
- Monotonicity: If one or several individuals move a durable up in their order of preference, this should be reflected in the order of preference of the "representative consumer."
- Composition condition: If groups of consumers who agree with each other are brought together, then the order of preferences of the "representative consumer" should not be affected.
- Labeling neutrality: If we relabel each durable good, the new names given to the durables should not affect the ordering of the "representative consumer."
- Independence condition: If a new durable good is introduced and either each individual buys it first or each individual buys it last, the order of preference for the original durables of the "representative consumer" should not be affected.
- Inversion condition: If rather than ordering the durable goods by ownership, we rank them by "non-ownership" the order of preference of the "representative consumer" should be identical to the inverse of the order of preference of the "representative consumer" for the owned durables.

Fine (1983) then proves that the order of preference of the "representative consumer" that obeys these six conditions is the Borda rule.

3.6 Comparing the Order of Acquisition with the Structure of Ownership

The idea here is to use a count approach and simply to compute the percentage of households that have no durable, one durable good, two durable goods, and so on. One then classifies these percentages by decreasing values and checks how different the ranking obtained is from the order of acquisition obtained using one of the methodologies that have been previously discussed.

4 Deriving the Order of Acquisition of Durable Goods and Assets: Empirical Illustrations

4.1 Introduction

This section is devoted to empirical studies aiming at discovering the order of acquisition of durable goods and assets. We first review the empirical literature. In Section 4.2 we focus our attention on papers that applied the approach of Paroush, while in Section 4.3 we review studies that used Item Response

Theory. Then in Section 4.4 we present a new empirical study based on data from the 2019 Eurobarometer survey. We first derive the order of acquisition obtained with each approach and then compare the two sets of results. Finally, we check to what extent the order of acquisition of a country depends on its standard of living.

4.2 Empirical Illustrations of the Order of Acquisition of Durable Goods or Financial Assets: The Approach of Guttman and Paroush

The paper by Kay (1964) seems to have been the first one to link the possession of durable goods to a Guttman scale. Kay examined data covering a single neighborhood (Manuhoe) of Papeete, the capital of French Polynesia. There were seven kinds of durable goods: a primus stove, a bicycle, a radio, a two-wheeled motor vehicle, a kerosene or gas stove, a refrigerator, and an automobile. This study covered only forty households and the most common order of acquisition was that following the order of durable goods in the list previously mentioned.

Paroush (1965) gives an illustration based on the 1961 Survey of Urban Families Expenditures in Israel and considers three durable goods: gas cooker, refrigerator, and washing machine. It turns out that 13 percent of the families owned the three durable goods, 32 percent a gas cooker and a refrigerator, 16 percent only a gas cooker, and 26 percent did not own any of these three durable goods. Looking at the deviations (12 percent of the sample) from the order "first gas cooker, then refrigerator, finally washing machine," Paroush observed that 7 percent owned only a refrigerator, 2 percent a refrigerator and a washing machine, 2 percent a gas cooker and a washing machine, and 1 percent only a washing machine. These results covered 99 percent of the sample so that, given that three durable gods were taken into account, the coefficient of Reproducibility R turns out to be expressed as

$$R = 1 - \left[\left(\frac{1}{3} \right) \left(\frac{12}{99} \right) \right] = 0.96$$

McFall (1969) also studied priority patterns in acquiring durable goods. He assumed that "consumers have sets of needs and values which are satisfied by sets of products, or, more correctly, by sets of product attributes." Such attributes could refer, for example, to "clean," "cook," "entertainment," "comfort," and so on. Using data obtained from a sample of upper income consumers in San Diego county, McFall considered the following four durable goods: automatic washer, electric blanket, dishwasher, air conditioner, and he found that this was the most common order of acquisition with 40 families owning all the four durables, 110 owning an automatic dishwasher, an electric blanket, and a dishwasher, 132 families owning only an automatic dishwasher and an electric blanket, 46 families owning only an automatic dishwasher, and 8 families not owning any of these four durable goods. There were 63 families that did not fit this order of acquisition (out of a total of 3999 families).

Kasulis et al. (1979) used data on consumer durables that were obtained for the years 1975 and 1976 from the Continuing Consumer Audit of the Distribution Research Program at the University of Oklahoma and the Oklahoma Publishing Company. Their analysis included 12 household durables and covered 1,747 respondents in 1975 and 2,025 in 1976. Using the Guttman scaling they concluded that in 1976 the order of acquisition was as follows: first TV, first vehicle, refrigerator, range, washer, stereo or tape player, dryer, second vehicle, second TV, dishwasher, freezer, and microwave oven. The order was almost the same in 1975. They also made a separate analysis for renters and owners, and it appears that the orders of acquisition were somewhat different in these two groups.

Stafford et al. (1982) used also the Guttman scaling to derive the order of acquisition by households of the following eight assets: corporate bonds, corporate stocks, checking accounts, husband's life insurance, mutual funds, savings accounts, trusts, and wife's life insurance. The data were also obtained for the years 1975 and 1976 from the Continuing Consumer Audit of the Distribution Research Program at the University of Oklahoma and the Oklahoma Publishing Company. For the full sample (about 3500 respondents) the order of acquisition obtained was as follows: Checking Account, Husband's Life Insurance, Savings Account, Wife's Life Insurance, Stocks, Bonds, Trust and Mutual Funds. The order obtained was quite similar when looking separately at three age groups: under thirty-five, thirty-five to forty-nine, and over fifty.

Clarke and Soutar (1982) analyzed a sample of 540 heads of households in the Perth (Australia) metropolitan area. The questions covered a list of fifteen durable goods and the order of acquisition obtained for the whole sample was as follows: Refrigerator, Washing machine, Vacuum cleaner, Color television, Power drill, Lawn-mover, Hi-fi stereo system, Deep-freeze unit, Air conditioner, Food processor, Clothes dryer, Video cassette recorder, Built-in swimming pool, Electric dishwasher, Microwave oven. The order was slightly different for owners and renters but very similar to that of the whole sample.

Dickson et al. (1983) used data from a 1978 Home Testing Institute screening survey of a panel of 5,000 households in the United States. Households were asked about the ownership of the following twelve appliances, and this is the order of acquisition obtained, using the Guttman scaling: Refrigerator, Clothes washer, Color TV, Sewing machine, Kitchen oven, Clothes dryer, Stereo AM/FM radio, Separate freezer, Dishwasher, Room air-conditioner, Microwave, and

Video Recorder. This order turns out to be identical to that obtained by classifying the appliances by the percentage of households that own them.

Dickinson and Kirzner (1986) focused their attention on the patterns of acquisition of financial assets. They used data from a survey carried out on behalf of a professional association in Canada. A questionnaire was sent out to each of the 36,044 members of this association and 14,569 questionnaires were returned. Ten financial assets were considered. Guttman's scalogram analysis revealed the following acquisition pattern: Checking account, Savings account, Husband insurance, RRSP (registered retirement savings plan), Wife insurance, Savings bonds, GIC (guaranteed investment certificates), Corporate stock, Mutual fund, and Corporate bond.

Deutsch and Silber (2008) used as database the 1995 Census of the Israeli population. This Census provides quite detailed information on the ownership of durable goods. Here are the durable goods that were taken into account in their study: telephone, television, washing machine, apartment (or house), VCR, car, microwave oven, air conditioner, dishwasher, computer, and dryer. Applying the approach of Paroush (1963), they observed that the most common order of acquisition of durable goods was that given by the list previously mentioned.

Bérenger et al. (2013) used data from the Demographic and Health Surveys (DHS) conducted in Egypt in 2005, in Morocco in 2003–2004 and in Turkey in 2003. The following durable goods and access to basic services were taken into account: ownership of dwelling, fuel for cooking, car, television, refrigerator, washing machine, video, phone, air conditioning, and type of toilet facilities. The orders of acquisition obtained, using the approach of Paroush (1963), were quite similar in the three countries. Thus in Egypt the order was: housing, cooking, toilet, TV, refrigerator, phone, washing machine, video, car, air conditioning. In Morocco the order was: housing, cooking, toilet, TV, phone, refrigerator, video, washing machine, car, and air conditioning. Finally in Turkey the order was: housing, TV, refrigerator, phone, toilet, washing machine, cooking, car, video, and air conditioning. Not surprisingly there were, however, differences between the orders observed in urban and rural areas.

Bérenger et al. (2016), applying the approach of Paroush (1963), analyzed data from samples of the 2000 and 2010 Mexican Censuses and derived the most common order of acquisition of durable goods in the various states of Mexico. In 2000, in most of the states, the most common order of importance seems to be toilet, television, radio, refrigerator, and washing machine. Then, depending on the states, they found hot water heater, car or phone, and finally computer. Quite similar patterns were observed in 2010. Thus the list of the four first goods remains the same, but in some states access to toilet becomes more essential in 2010 than in 2000.

Deutsch et al. (2020b) examined data on household consumer durables obtained from the Asian Barometer Survey for six countries of Southeast Asia: Cambodia, Indonesia, Malaysia, the Philippines, Thailand, and Vietnam. They applied the approach of Paroush and had data on the following eight assets: Car, jeep, or van; Color or black-and-white television; mobile phone; Electric fan or cooler; Scooter, motorcycle or bicycle; Radio transistor; Pumping Set; and Refrigerator. For the Philippines the order of acquisition obtained was as follows: TV, Fan/cooler, Transistor, Mobile phone, Refrigerator, Motorcycle, Pumping Set, and Car. For Thailand the order was: Fan/cooler, TV, Mobile phone, Motorcycle, Refrigerator, Transistor, Car, and Pumping Set. For Indonesia the order was: TV, Motorcycle, Mobile phone, Fan/cooler, Pumping Set, Refrigerator, Transistor, and Car. For Vietnam the order was: Motorcycle, TV, Fan/cooler, Mobile phone, Pumping Set, Refrigerator, Transistor, and Car. For Cambodia the order was: Motorcycle, TV, Mobile phone, Transistor, Fan/cooler, Pumping Set, Car, and Refrigerator. Finally for Malaysia the order was: Mobile phone, TV, Fan/cooler, Refrigerator, Motorcycle, Car, Transistor, and Pumping Set. Although the orders of acquisition vary from one country to the other, in many cases the correlation between the orders obtained in two countries was higher than 0.5 and often 0.6. But clearly the order reflects preferences for different durables, and preferences depend, among other factors, on culture, geographical conditions, and level of development.

Deutsch et al. (2020a) looked at data from the 2009 and 2013 Caucasus Barometer surveys and obtained information on the ownership of durable goods in Armenia, Azerbaijan, and Georgia. The following durable goods were taken account of: color TV, washing machine, refrigerator, air conditioner, car, cell phone, and personal computer. For 2013 the order of acquisition observed for Armenia was as follows: color TV, cell phone, refrigerator, washing machine, car, personal computer, and air conditioning. For Azerbaijan in 2013 the order was: cell phone, color TV, refrigerator, washing machine, car, air conditioning, and personal computer. Finally for Georgia the order in 2013 was: cell phone, color TV, refrigerator, washing machine, personal computer, car, and air conditioning. Note that the rank correlation between two countries was at least equal to 0.85 so that the orders of acquisition may be considered quite similar in the three countries examined.

Deutsch and Silber (2023) examined data obtained from the Eurobarometer for the year 2017. The data were available for thirty countries: France (1), Belgium (2), The Netherlands (3), West Germany (4), Italy (5), Luxembourg (6), Denmark (7), Ireland (8), Great Britain (9), Northern Ireland (10), Greece (11), Spain (12), Portugal (13), East Germany (14), Croatia (15), Finland (16), Sweden (17), Austria (18), Cyprus Republic (19), Czech Republic (20), Estonia

(21), Hungary (22), Latvia (23), Lithuania (24), Malta (25), Poland (26), Slovakia (27), Slovenia (28), Bulgaria (29), and Romania (30). The following information was available concerning the durables and services available in the households: Phone (Good 1), Mobile Phone (Good 2), Television (Good 3), DVD (Good 4), CD player (Good 5), Computer (Good 6), Laptop (Good 7), Tablet (Good 8), Smartphone (Good 9), Internet (Good 10), Car (Good 11), and House which is already paid for (Good 12). We will not give the orders of acquisition obtained, using the Paroush approach, for each of these thirty countries. But it is interesting to note that Deutsch and Silber (2023) regressed the rank correlation between the orders of acquisition of two countries on the absolute value of the difference between the equalized median incomes of these two countries. They found that the coefficient of the absolute value of this difference was negative and significant and the R-squared of this regression was equal to 0.46.

4.3 Empirical Illustrations of the Order of Acquisition of Durable Goods or Financial Assets: Using Item Response Theory

Although Item Response Theory (IRT) was originally used in psychometrics, this technique has also been used to measure deprivation, the idea being that poverty, like intelligence, is really a latent variable that is difficult to measure.

Let us first assume that deprivation is unidimensional. Deprivation, however, cannot be observed as it is a latent variable. What we observe is a distribution of a certain number of binary deprivation indicators observed for, say, n households or individuals. A simple way of estimating overall deprivation would be to assume that it is equal to the unweighted or weighted sum of all the dichotomous indicators. In the latter case one could assume, for example, that a higher weight is given to an indicator, the lower its prevalence, the idea being that if not many households (individuals) do not have a given item, this item should not contribute much to the overall level of deprivation.

Assume we give the same weight to all the deprivation indicators. Then the value IND_{jh} taken by indicator h for individual j could be expressed as

$$IND_{jh} = LD_j + u_{jh}$$

where LD_j refers to the value of the latent deprivation for individual j, while u_{jh} is an error term assumed to have zero mean and to be independent of LD_j. These error terms are also assumed to be mutually independent. It is then easy to observe, if the number of deprivation indicators is large enough, that the average value of the deprivation indicators for individual j will be equal to the value of the latent deprivation for this individual.

The problem is that these deprivation indicators are dichotomous and not continuous variables so that this approach to measuring latent deprivation cannot be adopted, hence the idea to use Item Response Theory.

The first applications of Item Response Theory to the analysis of poverty seem to have been the studies of Dickes (1983), Dickes et al. (1984) and Gailly and Hausman (1984). They used the Rasch model, estimating a unique parameter per item, the one which measures the "difficulty." Therefore, all the items have the same slope as far as the relationship between poverty and the probability of having a disadvantage is concerned. Poverty is hence defined as an accumulation of disadvantages.

Soutar and Cornish-Ward (1997) analyzed data on durable and financial asset ownership. These data were collected in 1989 in the area of Perth in Western Australia, by a commercial social research organization using telephone interviews. The authors applied the Rasch model using information on the ownership of twenty-five durable goods. The Rasch model ranked them in the following order: refrigerator, vacuum cleaner, washing machine, first color TV, toaster, first car, power tools, electric fan, Hi-Fi/video, video recorder, microwave oven, lawn lower, deep freezer, second car, food processor, clothes dryer, second color TV, electric shaver, small-food heater, large space heater, air conditioner, juicer, solar hot water heater, computer, and car phone.

For financial assets the Rasch model gave the following order: savings account, property home, checking account, superannuation, life insurance, shares, fixed deposits in bank, fixed deposits in credit society, other property, cash management trust, equity trust, collectables, insurance bonds, government bonds, and debentures.

Capellari and Jenkins (2007) used data from wave 6 (survey year 1996) of the British Household Panel Survey (BHPS). Their focus was on "basic life-style" deprivation and they used seven binary indicator variables. The first six variables asked whether the households were able to keep their home adequately warm, eat meat, chicken, fish every second day, buy new, rather than second hand, clothes, have friends or family for a drink or meal at least once a month, replace worn-out furniture, and pay for a week's annual holiday away from home. The seventh binary indicator variable asked whether the responding household had any difficulties paying for their accommodation in the last twelve months. When using a one-parameter model, the results were very similar to those obtained when looking at the frequency of each of the seven deprivation aspects analyzed, namely that having difficulties paying for the accommodation is the most common deprivation, followed by the difficulty of taking a week's vacation, and so on. Capellari and Jenkins (2007) found similar results when using a two-parameter IRT model.

Dickes and Fusco (2008) also applied the Rasch model. Their empirical illustration was based on the EU-SILC data. Luxembourg was part of the countries that launched their survey in 2003, and the initial sample of PSELL-3 (*Panel Socio-Economique "Liewen zu Lëtzebuerg"*) consisted of 3,500 representative households (9500 individuals). Dickes and Fusco used the data relative to the second wave of PSELL-3, conducted in 2004. They selected a set of items referring to the absence of housing facilities, to problems with the accommodation, to problems with the environment or neighborhood, to the inability to afford most basic requirements, to the inability to meet payment schedules, and to the lack of durable goods. A list of twenty-nine dichotomous items was originally selected, and for every item, an estimation of severity parameter was obtained. Dickes and Fusco then focused their attention on the following nine durable goods: color TV, computer, washing machine, private car, camera, video player, CD player, DVD player, and audio tape player. They then concluded that the following items fit the Rasch model assumptions: the possession of a video player, a camera, a private car, a washing machine, and a color TV. This is the order given by the severity (location) parameter, implying that this is the sequence of acquisition of these five durable goods. Dickes and Fusco also analyzed other deprivation domains such as financial difficulties and problems with the environment.

Raileanu Szeles and Fusco (2013) applied IRT models to measure deprivation and analyze its determinants in Luxembourg. Their analysis used data from the Socio-Economic Panel "Liewen zu Lëtzebuerg" (PSELL-3), which is the Luxembourgish component of the EU Community Statistics on Income and Living Conditions (EU-SILC). Nine dichotomous items pertaining to the enforced lack of durable goods, housing facilities, and the capacity to afford basic requirements were taken account of. The items are listed below according to their increasing deprivation rates in Luxembourg computed on 3,001 observations: cannot afford to have a washing machine (if wanted to), the dwelling has no bath, cannot afford keeping home adequately warm, cannot afford to have a car (if wanted to), cannot afford eating meat or equivalent every second day, cannot afford one-week annual holiday away from home, and cannot afford facing unexpected expenses. Raileanu Szeles and Fusco estimated a one- and a two-parameter IRT model and this allowed them to rank the items of deprivation according to their parameter of severity. The items "washing machine" and "bath" were the most severe in the one-parameter IRT, implying that the probability that an individual who has no bath (or no washing machine) will be deprived of the other items is higher than 0.5. When using the two-parameter IRT models, the item "washing machine" is again the most difficult item, whereas the rank of the "bath" was lower than in the one-parameter model.

The ability to face unexpected expenses is the easiest item in both models. Note also that the one- and two-parameter models yield different rankings of deprivation items in terms of their difficulty, a result which is different from what Cappellari and Jenkins (2007) had found.

Dholakia and Banerjee (2013) used data provided by Pathfinders, a research group based in Mumbai, India, that regularly surveys households on various consumption related attitudes and behaviors. The datasets contained 2,864 respondents in 1996, and 2,686 respondents in 2002, drawn from the western part of India. The authors used the two-parameter Item Response Theory to detect the priority pattern in the acquisition of household durables. In 1996 the list of durables was as follows: radio, pressure cooker, ceiling fans, color TV, food processor, sewing machine, refrigerator, cassette player, Two in One, video, washing machine, stereo, Air conditioning, vacuum cleaner, and cooking range. The priority followed this order so that a radio had the highest priority and a cooking range the lowest.

In 2002 the priorities were as follows: pressure cooker, food processor, refrigerator, telephone, washing machine, Hi-Fi, mobile, video, air conditioner, computer, DVD/CD player, sewing machine, oven, radio, dishwasher, Two in One, and cooking range. The authors stressed the fact that by 2002, the hierarchy had become somewhat similar to the pattern of durable ownership observed in countries like Israel (see Paroush, 1965).

Deutsch, Guio, and Pomati (2015) used Item Response Theory to estimate the extent of material deprivation in twenty-seven European Union countries, using the EU-SILC 2009 data. As mentioned previously, this database was also used to apply the Paroush approach. The focus here was on the order of curtailment of expenditures when households start facing poverty. The expenditures in this analysis were the following ones: holidays, unexpected expenses, furniture, pocket money, leisure, drink/meal out, clothes, meat/chicken/fish, keeping the home warm, arrears, car, computer/Internet, and shoes. IRT analysis showed that, for the European Union as a whole, the sequence of curtailment of expenditures followed the order of the items that was just mentioned. In most countries a one-week holiday away from home is always one of the first three types of expenditures to be curtailed, together with the ability to face unexpected expenses. On the other hand, two pairs of all-weather shoes are at least the eighth item to be given up and "computer/Internet" at least the ninth item. Finally note that the orders of expenditures curtailment are very similar to those obtained when using the Paroush approach.

Bérenger, Deutsch, and Silber (2016) applied Item Response Theory to Mexican Census data for the years 2000 and 2010, as they did when applying the Paroush approach (see Section 4.2) to these data. They selected the same nine assets, namely a phone, a car, a hot water heater, a computer, a washing machine, a refrigerator, a television, a radio, and a toilet. These authors then found that the order derived from IRT was almost the same as that obtained with the Paroush approach, this being true for almost all the Mexican states. Thus, in 2000, in every state, the first items were access to toilet, television, radio, refrigerator, washing machine, while the last one was a computer. Small differences between the two approaches were observed mainly when looking at the ranking of the three last goods in the order of acquisition. This ranking similarity between the IRT and the Paroush approach was also observed when analyzing the 2010 Census.

Deutsch et al. (2020b) applied Item Response Theory to the database they had used when applying the Paroush approach, namely the 2014 and 2016 Asian Barometer Survey (ABS). Here also they focused their attention on six countries in Southeast Asia (Cambodia, Indonesia, Malaysia, the Philippines, Thailand, and Vietnam) and eight durable goods (car, jeep or van; color or black-and-white television; mobile phone; electric fan or cooler; scooter, motorcycle or bicycle; radio transistor; pumping set; and refrigerator). They then computed the rank correlations between the countries. It turned out that ten of the fifteen correlations were higher than 0.5 and 8 higher than 0.6. The highest correlation observed was between Vietnam and Indonesia. Thailand and Malaysia also exhibited similar orders of acquisition. But the correlation between the rankings of Cambodia and Malaysia was low (0.12). It is clear that the order of preferences depends on the level of development but also on culture, geographical conditions, and other factors.

Deutsch, Silber, Xu, and Wan (2020) applied Item Response Theory to the 2009 and 2013 Caucasus Barometer surveys which provided information on the ownership of durable goods in Armenia, Azerbaijan, and Georgia. These authors used the same list of durable goods they had selected when applying the Paroush approach (see Section 4.2), namely a color TV, a washing machine, a refrigerator, an air conditioner, a car, a cell phone, and a personal computer. For each of the three countries examined they found a very high correlation (above 0.85) between the order of acquisition obtained when adopting the Paroush approach and that derived when using Item Response Theory. The correlation between the orders obtained when comparing two countries was very high also (at least equal to 0.92).

Farcomeni et al. (2022), using the Rasch model analytical procedure, derived from the Survey on Income and Living Conditions (EU-SILC) pre-Covid data, a European measurement reference scale for material deprivation which ensures validity and comparability across different countries. Their analysis included originally twenty-three items collected at both the household and individual level. However, they ended up working with eight items to guarantee uni-dimensionality. Here is the list of the eight items ranked by increasing severity:

- The household cannot afford to face unexpected expenses.
- The person cannot afford to spend a small amount of money each week on himself/herself.
- The household has arrears on mortgage, rent, utility bills or loans.
- The person cannot afford to get-together with friends/family (relatives) for a drink/meal at least once a month.
- The household cannot afford a meal with meat, chicken and fish (or vegetarian equivalent) every second day.
- The person cannot afford to have Internet connection for personal use at home.
- The person cannot afford medical examination or treatment.
- The household has not a telephone (including mobile phone).

Deutsch and Silber (2023) applied Item Response Theory to the same 2017 Eurobarometer database they had used to examine the Paroush approach to the order of acquisition of durable goods. Their analysis covered the same thirty countries and included the same twelve durable goods mentioned in Section 4.2. For each country, they therefore derived the ranking of the different goods and compared these rankings with that obtained when using the Paroush approach. More precisely they computed for each country the correlation coefficient between the set of rank correlations derived when using the Paroush approach and that obtained when implementing Item Response Theory and found that this coefficient of correlation was at least equal to 0.9, except for Spain, where it was equal to 0.87. They then regressed the rank correlation between the orders of acquisition of two countries on the absolute value of the difference between the equalized median incomes of the two countries compared. The coefficient of the absolute value of this difference was negative and significant, and the R-squared of this regression was equal to 0.50.

4.4 Comparing the Different Approaches to the Derivation of the Order of Acquisition of Durable Goods: A New Study

This empirical investigation is based on data from the 2019 Eurobarometer survey. We apply the Rasch model (see Section 3.4 for more details on Item Response Theory and the Rasch model). We used data covering thirty-five countries: France (1), Belgium (2), The Netherlands (3), Former West Germany (4), Italy (5), Luxembourg (6), Denmark (7), Ireland (8), United Kingdom (9) Greece (10), Spain (11), Portugal (12), Former East Germany (13), Finland (14),

Sweden (15), Austria (16), Cyprus Republic (17), Czech Republic (18), Estonia (19), Hungary (20), Latvia (21), Lithuania (22), Malta (23), Poland (24), Slovakia (25), Slovenia (26), Bulgaria (27), Romania (28). Turkey (29), Croatia (30), Cyprus TCC(31), North Macedonia (32), Montenegro (33), Serbia (34), and Albania (35).

The following information was available concerning the durables and services available in the households: Phone (Good 1), Mobile Phone (Good 2), Television (Good 3), DVD (Good 4), CD player (Good 5), Computer (Good 6), Laptop (Good 7), Tablet (Good 8), Smartphone (Good 9), Internet (Good 10), Car (Good 11), and House which is already paid for (Good 12).

Table 4 gives the most common order of acquisition for each of the thirty-five countries under study, when using the Paroush approach. The columns indicate which good (or service) has the first, second, third rank, and so on. Table 5 is similar to Table 4, but it is derived from Item Response Theory.

We can then use each of these two tables to compute, for each binary comparison of countries, the rank correlation between two countries in the order of acquisition of these goods or services. These correlations are presented in Appendix B in Table B.1 for the Paroush approach and in Table B.2 for the approach based on Item Response Theory. We observe a great variety of values for these correlation coefficients as some correlations are quite low (less than 0.2) and some others very high (close to 1). A quick look at these correlations seems to indicate that the correlations are much higher when the two countries compared are of a somewhat similar development level. This was confirmed by a regression analysis, which will be mentioned below.

We then computed for each of the thirty-five countries on which we had information the correlation coefficient between the order of acquisition derived from the Paroush approach and that obtained when implementing Item Response Theory. These correlations are presented in Table 6. It turns out that this coefficient of correlation was never below 0.85, most of the time above 0.9, if not 0.95. Therefore, it does not seem to matter very much whether we use the Paroush approach or Item Response Theory to derive the most common order of acquisition of these goods and services.

Finally, we regressed the rank correlation between the orders of acquisition of two countries on the absolute value of the difference between the per capita GDP of these two countries. One regression was based on the rank correlation derived from the Paroush approach and the other from that obtained with Item Response Theory. These regressions are given in Table 7. It turns out that the coefficient of the absolute value of this per capita GDP difference is negative and significant, and the R-squared of this regression is equal to 0.38 when using the Paroush approach and to 0.46 when implementing Item Response Theory.

Table 4 Order of Acquisition using the Paroush approach

	1	2	3	4	5	6	7	8	9	10	11	12	Reproducibility Index
France	3	2	1	11	10	9	7	8	6	4	5	12	0.8689
Belgium	2	3	10	9	7	11	8	4	5	6	1	12	0.8651
Netherlands	1	10	2	3	11	9	7	8	4	5	6	12	0.9274
West Germany	2	3	1	11	10	9	7	4	5	8	6	12	0.8816
Italy	3	2	9	11	10	7	8	1	12	4	5	6	0.8653
Luxembourg	2	3	11	10	9	7	8	1	4	5	6	12	0.8921
Denmark	2	3	10	9	7	11	8	4	5	6	1	12	0.9166
Ireland	2	3	11	9	10	7	8	4	5	1	6	12	0.8905
United Kingdom	3	2	10	9	7	8	11	1	4	5	6	12	0.8789
Greece	3	2	1	12	11	10	9	7	4	5	8	6	0.8984
Spain	3	2	1	11	9	10	7	8	6	4	5	12	0.8775
Portugal	3	2	1	11	10	9	7	8	4	5	12	6	0.9005
East Germany	3	2	1	11	9	10	7	4	5	8	6	12	0.8687
Finland	2	3	11	10	7	9	8	5	4	6	12	1	0.8968
Sweden	2	10	9	7	3	11	8	5	4	6	1	12	0.8934
Austria	3	2	11	9	10	7	4	8	5	6	12	1	0.8800
Cyprus Republic	3	12	2	11	1	10	9	8	7	5	4	6	0.8954
Czech Republic	2	3	10	9	11	7	4	5	8	6	12	1	0.8787

Table 4 (cont.)

	1	2	3	4	5	6	7	8	9	10	11	12	Reproducibility Index
Estonia	2	3	12	10	7	9	11	6	8	4	5	1	0.8918
Hungary	3	12	2	9	10	7	11	6	4	5	1	8	0.8833
Latvia	2	3	12	10	9	7	11	6	8	4	5	1	0.8848
Lithuania	3	2	12	11	10	7	9	8	6	5	4	1	0.9090
Malta	3	1	12	2	11	10	9	7	8	6	4	5	0.9208
Poland	2	3	12	11	10	7	9	8	4	5	6	1	0.8957
Slovakia	3	12	2	11	10	9	7	8	6	4	5	1	0.8986
Slovenia	2	3	12	11	10	9	7	8	6	5	4	1	0.8913
Bulgaria	3	12	2	11	9	10	7	8	6	4	5	1	0.9016
Romania	3	2	12	9	10	11	7	8	6	4	5	1	0.9263
Turkey	2	3	9	10	7	11	12	8	6	4	5	1	0.9073
Croatia	3	2	9	12	11	10	7	1	8	6	4	5	0.8820
Cyprus (Turkish Cypriot Community)	3	2	10	9	1	11	12	7	6	8	4	5	0.8985
North Macedonia	3	2	12	9	10	11	7	6	1	4	5	8	0.8770
Montenegro	3	2	9	10	12	11	7	8	1	6	4	5	0.8875
Serbia	3	2	12	1	9	10	6	11	7	8	4	5	0.8779
Albania	2	3	9	12	4	11	6	10	7	1	5	8	0.8946

Note: For France commodity 3 is first in path of acquisition, commodity 2 second, and so on.

Table 5 Order of Acquisition derived from Item Response Theory

	1	2	3	4	5	6	7	8	9	10	11	12	Number of observations
France	3	2	10	11	9	1	7	4	8	5	6	12	1,013
Belgium	2	3	10	9	11	7	8	5	4	1	12	6	1,057
Netherlands	1	10	2	3	11	9	7	8	5	4	6	12	1,020
West Germany	2	3	1	10	9	11	7	4	5	6	8	12	1,035
Italy	3	2	9	11	10	7	1	12	8	4	5	6	1,026
Luxembourg	2	3	11	10	9	1	7	4	8	5	6	12	506
Denmark	2	3	10	9	11	7	8	4	5	6	1	12	1,013
Ireland	2	3	9	10	11	7	8	4	5	1	12	6	1,028
United Kingdom	3	2	10	9	1	11	7	8	4	5	12	6	1,032
Greece	3	2	1	11	10	9	12	7	4	5	8	6	1,012
Spain	3	2	9	10	11	1	7	12	8	6	4	5	1,007
Portugal	3	2	10	11	9	1	7	8	12	4	5	6	1,008
East Germany	3	2	1	9	11	10	4	7	5	6	12	8	452
Finland	2	3	10	11	9	7	5	4	8	12	6	1	1,004
Sweden	2	10	3	9	7	11	5	8	4	6	1	12	1,015
Austria	3	2	11	9	10	4	7	5	8	6	12	1	1,022
Cyprus Republic	3	2	11	10	9	12	1	8	7	5	4	6	505
Czech Republic	2	3	10	9	11	7	4	12	5	8	6	1	1004

Table 5 (cont.)

	1	2	3	4	5	6	7	8	9	10	11	12	Number of observations
Estonia	2	3	12	10	9	11	7	6	8	1	5	4	1,003
Hungary	3	2	9	10	12	11	7	4	6	1	5	8	1,038
Latvia	2	3	10	9	12	7	11	6	8	4	5	1	1,016
Lithuania	3	2	12	10	9	11	7	8	6	5	1	4	1,006
Malta	3	2	1	11	12	10	9	7	8	6	4	5	503
Poland	2	3	10	9	11	7	12	4	8	6	5	1	1,000
Slovakia	3	2	12	11	10	9	7	6	8	4	5	1	1,058
Slovenia	2	3	11	10	9	12	7	1	6	8	5	4	1,011
Bulgaria	3	2	12	11	9	10	7	6	8	1	4	5	1,031
Romania	3	2	12	9	10	11	7	8	6	1	4	5	1,025
Turkey	2	3	9	10	7	11	8	12	6	4	1	5	1,008
Croatia	3	2	9	11	10	12	7	1	6	8	4	5	1,014
Cyprus (Turkish Cypriot Community)	3	2	10	9	11	1	12	7	6	8	4	5	500
North Macedonia	3	2	9	10	12	11	6	7	1	4	5	8	1,017
Montenegro	3	2	9	10	12	11	7	8	1	6	4	5	532
Serbia	3	2	12	1	9	10	11	7	6	8	4	5	998
Albania	2	3	9	12	11	4	10	6	5	7	1	8	1,005

Note: For France commodity 3 is first in path of acquisition, commodity 2 second, and so on.

Table 6 Rank Correlation between the orders based on
the Paroush approach and those derived from Item
Response Theory

Country	Correlation Coefficient
France	0.916
Belgium	0.965
Netherlands	0.993
West Germany	0.972
Italy	0.979
Luxembourg	0.965
Denmark	0.993
Ireland	0.972
United Kingdom	0.930
Greece	0.958
Spain	0.867
Portugal	0.930
East Germany	0.965
Finland	0.958
Sweden	0.972
Austria	0.986
Cyprus Republic	0.895
Czech Republic	0.958
Estonia	0.951
Hungary	0.937
Latvia	0.979
Lithuania	0.958
Malta	0.965
Poland	0.881
Slovakia	0.986
Slovenia	0.881
Bulgaria	0.965
Romania	0.979
Turkey	0.986
Croatia	0.972
Cyprus (Turkish Cypriot Community)	0.993
North Macedonia	0.972
Montenegro	1.000
Serbia	0.979
Albania	0.965

Table 7 Regressing the rank correlation between the orders of acquisition of two countries and the absolute gap between their per capita GDP

	The approach of Paroush	Item Response Theory
Constant	0.969	0.994
	(14.1)	(22.2)
Absolute value of the gap in per capita GDP of two countries	−0.00000954	−0.00000666
	(−9.34)	(−9.96)
R-squared	0.380	0.476
F-value	7.65	11.3
Number of observations	378	378

Note: t-values in parenthesis.

Note that in estimating these regressions we took account of the fact that we work with dyadic regressions. As stressed by Cameron and Miller (2014), regression models with paired or dyadic data have a complicated pattern of error correlations. Cameron and Miller (2014) observed that even after including country fixed effects, standard errors that properly control for dyadic error correlation can be several times those being reported using regular methods.[13]

4.5 Concluding Comments

Two main conclusions may be drawn from the new empirical investigation that was conducted in this section. First, it probably does not matter whether the order of acquisition of durable goods and assets is derived via the use of the Paroush approach or using Item Response Theory. Both techniques seem to lead to very similar results. Second, the order of acquisition of durable goods and assets depends, at least partly, on the standard of living of a country since we found that the rank correlation between the orders of acquisition of two countries is a negative and significant function of the absolute gap between the per capita GDP of these two countries. This leads one to conclude that the order of acquisition of durable goods and assets could be considered as a proxy for the standard of living of a country although clearly other factors, such as geographical and cultural considerations, most likely have also an impact on such an order of acquisition.

---

[13] For more details on dyadic regressions see chapter 2 in Graham (2020).

5 The Order of Acquisition of Durable Goods and Assets and the Measurement of Inequality, Poverty, and Welfare

5.1 Introduction

In this section we show that deriving the order of acquisition of durable goods and assets may allow one to draw conclusions concerning the extent of inequality and poverty in a country and even to compare the levels of welfare in different countries. This is possible because such an order of acquisition tells us which percentage of the individuals (households) surveyed have no durable good, one, two, three . . ., all the durable goods. This information then allows one to estimate the extent of inequality and poverty in a country, given that important work has shown in recent years how to obtain measures of inequality and poverty when only ordinal variables are available. It is even possible to estimate the extent of welfare, using recent work deriving achievement indices that also take account of the inequality of achievements. This recent literature focusing on ordinal variables is reviewed in Section 5.2 for the measurement of inequality, in Section 5.3 for the derivation of poverty indices, and in Section 5.4 for the estimation of achievement indices, and more generally of welfare. Finally, in Section 5.5 an empirical illustration, based again on data from the 2019 Eurobarometer Survey, is presented where the different inequality, poverty, and achievement indices are computed for the various countries that participated to this survey.

5.2 Ordinal Variables and the Measurement of Inequality

In a pathbreaking article, Allison and Foster (2004) stressed the fact that traditional measures of inequality, such as the Gini coefficient, the index of Atkinson (1970), the entropy-related measures introduced by Theil (1967), or the variance, are based on the mean since in one way or the other they turn out to be deviations from the mean or they are indices which are normalized by the mean. However, when the variable under study is ordinal, the notion of mean is not well defined. Allison and Foster (2004), taking self-assessed health, an ordinal variable, as illustration, showed that in measuring health inequality in different populations, via traditional inequality indices, completely different results could be obtained, depending on the scale chosen for the ordinal categories.

This is the reason why Allison and Foster (2004) advocated a median-based approach. They then defined what they called a S-curve,[14] which allows ranking distributions of ordinal variables in the same way as the Lorenz curve represents the Lorenz ranking of income distributions. The S-curve, like the Lorenz curve, gives only a partial ordering since when two S-curves cross, no conclusion may

---

[14] See their paper for more details on the way they construct this S-curve.

be drawn. The authors then indicated that several useful indexes of "spread" can be derived from the S-curve in the same way as the Gini index may be derived from the Lorenz curve.

Three years later, in a quite original article, Apouey (2007) noted that the literature on polarization (see Wolfson, 1994; Esteban and Ray, 1994; Duclos et al., 2004) also puts the emphasis on the median. This literature deals, however, with cardinal variables, but the two principles that it stresses are also relevant in the case of ordinal variables, as will be shown in the next paragraphs.

The first principle (increasing spread) states that moving from the middle position (the median) to the tails of the distribution will make the distribution more polarized. In the case of a cardinal variable such as income, this principle implies that a rank-preserving increment in incomes above the median or a rank-preserving reduction in income below the median will widen the distribution, that is, increase the distance between the group of individuals whose income is smaller than the median income and the group of people whose income is higher than the median income. Consequently, polarization in society will increase because the rich become richer and the poor poorer.

The second principle is called increased bipolarity. It refers to the case where the incomes below the median or those above the median become closer to each other. The literature on polarization states then that there has been some "bunching" of the two groups; that is, the gaps between the incomes below the median (or those above the median) have been reduced. If this is so, bipolarization is said to increase.

It should therefore be clear that there is an important difference between the notions of "inequality" and "bipolarization." While any regressive transfer will increase inequality, it will increase bipolarization only in the case where such a transfer takes place across the median. When it takes place on the same side of the median, bipolarization will decrease.

Apouey (2007) used these two principles of increased spread and bipolarity to derive polarization indices that could be used in the case of ordinal variables. Moreover, the transfer principle was interpreted, in the case of ordinal variables, as implying a movement of individuals from one category to another. Apouey (2007) also indicated that such a polarization index should vary between 0 and 1. Taking as illustration the order of acquisition of durable goods, it is assumed that there is no polarization when everyone has the same number of durable goods and polarization will be maximal (the index being equal to 1) when half the population owns no durable good and the other half has all the durable goods.

Assume $(K + 1)$ categories so that $k = 0$ corresponds to the case where an individual does not own any durable good while $k = K$ refers to the case where the individual owns all the K durable goods. The ordinal inequality index Apouey proposed is then defined as

$$I_{APOUEY} = 1 - \frac{2^{\alpha}}{K} \sum\nolimits_{k=0}^{K} \left| P_k - 0.5 \right|^{\alpha} \tag{13}$$

where P_k refers to the cumulative frequency corresponding to the case when k durable goods are owned. Note that Apouey suggested to calibrate α in such a way that it will be equal to 0.5 in the case of a uniform distribution (the case where there is the same number of individuals in each of the possibilities considered, that is from $k = 0$ to $k = K$). The idea is that a uniform distribution is a kind of intermediate state between the extreme cases where polarization is minimal or maximal. Apouey then listed some other useful properties of her index.[15]

In another important paper Abul Naga and Yalcin (2008) characterized the entire class of inequality indices founded on the ordering defined by Allison and Foster. The ordinal inequality measures they derived have also the property that inequality is maximal when half of the population is in the lowest category and the other half is in the highest one. These ordinal inequality indices were shown by the authors to satisfy the properties of continuity, scale invariance, normalization, and aversion to median preserving spreads.[16]

Taking again as illustration the order of acquisition of durable goods, let p_k be the proportion of individuals in category k. Assume that the various categories are ordered by increasing number of durable goods owned. Define then P_k as the cumulative values of the probabilities p_k, that is,

$P_k = p_0 + p_1 + \ldots + p_k$. The first ordinal inequality index suggested by Abul Naga and Yalcin is then defined as

$$I_{ABU\ NAGA\ YALCIN} = 1 - \left[\frac{\left(2 \sum_{k=0}^{K} \left| P_k - 0.5 \right| - 1 \right)}{K} \right] \tag{14}$$

Note that this index $I_{ABU\ NAGA\ YALCIN}$ has the four properties mentioned previously.

Abul Naga and Yalcin introduced then a generalization of the index defined in (14), which depends on two parameters. These two parameters allow one to assume asymmetry, that is, to obtain different results when a given deviation from 0.5 take place below or above the median.[17]

Kobus and Milos (2012) also proposed a generalization of the index introduced by Abul Naga and Yalcin (2008).[18]

---

[15] See her paper for more details.
[16] See the paper by Abul Naga and Yalcin (2008) for an explanation of these properties.
[17] See their paper for the exact formulation for the generalization of the index $I_{ABU\ NAGA\ YALCIN}$ defined in (5.2).
[18] See their paper for more details on their index.

Another approach was taken by Reardon (2009). The focus of his analysis was on the measurement of ordinal segregation. However, it turns out that these measures may also be used to measure ordinal inequality (see Lazar and Silber, 2013). As before, let $(K + 1)$ refer to the number of categories (remember that $k = 0$ corresponds to the case where an individual does not own any durable good(. Define then a function v as

$$v = \left(\frac{1}{K}\right)\sum_{k=0}^{K-1} f(P_k) \tag{15}$$

Reardon (2009) introduces then the following four functions $f(P_k)$:

$$f_1(P_k) = -[P_k log_2 P_k + (1 - P_k) log_2 (1 - P_k)] \tag{16}$$

$$f_2(P_k) = 4P_k(1 - P_k) \tag{17}$$

$$f_3(P_k) = 2\sqrt{P_k(1 - P_k)} \tag{18}$$

$$f_4(P_k) = 1 - |2P_k - 1| \tag{19}$$

If we combine (15) with one of the four functions defined in equations (16) to (19), we obtain, in fact, measures of ordinal inequality which satisfy the four desirable properties stressed by Abul Naga and Yalcin (2008): continuity, scale invariance, normalization, and aversion to median preserving spreads. Note that it can be shown that the index proposed by Abul Naga and Yalcin (2008) in (13) is, in fact, a combination of (15) and (19).

Lazar and Silber (2013) combined the approach of Reardon (2009) with the generalization of the index introduced by Abul Naga and Yalcin to derive another measure of ordinal inequality.[19]

Lv et al. (2015) took a somewhat different approach to the measurement of ordinal inequality. Taking again the case of the order of acquisition of durables as illustration,[20] these authors first proposed a measure of the inequality between any two durables ownership categories. Then, in a second stage, these inequalities are aggregated via a weighted sum, in which the further apart the two durables ownership categories are, the higher the weight attached to the inequality between these two ownership categories. In fact, Lv et al. (2015) derived axiomatically two ordinal inequality indices. The first one is expressed as

---

[19] See the paper of Lazar and Silber (2013) for more details.
[20] The paper of Lv et al. (2015) used health inequality as illustration.

$$I_{LWX1} = \sum_{k=0}^{K} \sum_{j \neq k} \left(\frac{2}{K}\right) |k - j| f_k f_j \tag{20}$$

where, as before, $(K + 1)$ is the number of possible durables ownership categories and f_k and f_j are the proportions of individuals belonging to ownership categories k and j.

The second index that Lv et al. (2015) proposed is defined as

$$I_{LWX2} = \sum_{k=0}^{K} \sum_{j \neq k} {}^{K-|k-j|} f_k f_j \tag{21}$$

with $0 << 1$

Lv et al. (2015) showed that the two previous indices obey a certain number of desirable axioms.[21]

Cowell and Flachaire (2017) took a completely different approach to the measurement of ordinal inequality, one that is based on the notion of "status." The idea is to link a categorical data structure to the notion of "status." More precisely, the approach of Cowell and Flachaire includes three main elements: the notion of status within a distribution, a reference point, and a set of axioms. Note that in their view status can be downward- or upward-looking, depending on the context of the analysis. These authors characterize then a family of indices that depends on a sensitivity parameter and a reference point. This reference point can be either the maximal or the minimal possible value of the status.[22]

5.3 Measuring Poverty with Ordinal Variables: The Counting Approach

Following Sen (1976), the traditional approach to unidimensional poverty measurement makes a distinction between an identification and aggregation stage. First a decision needs to be made concerning the way an individual will be classified as poor or non-poor. Then this information is aggregated to derive an overall measure of poverty.

However, in a multidimensional approach to poverty measurement there will be three and not two stages. First, for each variable, it is necessary to decide whether the individual or household is deprived with respect to this variable. If the focus of the analysis is on the number of durable goods or assets owned, the answer to such a question will be easy to derive since the individual either owns the durable good or asset under study, or he/she

---

[21] See their paper for more details on these axioms.
[22] For more details see Cowell and Flachaire (2017).

does not. In a second stage, it is necessary to determine the number of durable goods or assets which an individual or a household needs to own to be considered as "not deprived" or "not poor." Finally, in a third stage, the conclusions reached for each individual (whether he/she is "poor" or not) will be aggregated to derive an overall measure of the extent of multidimensional poverty in the society.

The Alkire and Foster (2011) Approach with Dichotomous Variables

Given the available data on the ownership of various assets, one may wonder how to aggregate such an information (individuals either own or do not own a given asset) to obtain an overall measure of poverty. There are in fact several ways of looking at this issue. First there is the so-called "union" approach. It assumes that the various assets are perfect complements, so that, as soon as one asset is missing, the individual or household will be considered as poor. The intersection approach, on the contrary, assumes that the assets are perfect substitutes, so that an individual or a household will be considered as poor only if he/she does not own any asset. Alkire and Foster (2011) proposed an intermediate approach, where, given that K refers to the total number of assets, an individual (or household) will be considered as poor only if the number of assets he/she owns is smaller than or equal to $k_{critical}$, with $1 \leq k_{critical} \leq K$.

Now let H refer to the proportion of individuals or households defined as "poor." Let N refer to the total number of individuals (households) and N_P to the number of poor. H is then computed as

$$H = \left(\frac{N_P}{N}\right) \tag{22}$$

Among those N_P individuals (households) considered as poor, let A refer to the proportion of assets that these poor individuals (households) do not have. Let $I(x_{ik})$ be equal to 1 if individual (household) i does not have asset k, to 0 otherwise. We may then write that

$$A = \frac{\left\{\sum_{i=1}^{N_P}\left[\sum_{k=1}^{K}\frac{I(x_{ik})}{K}\right]\right\}}{N_P} \tag{23}$$

Alkire and Foster (2011) combined the two indicators H and A to define a "dimension adjusted headcount ratio" M_0 where

$$M_0 = H \times A = \left(\frac{N_P}{N}\right)\left\{\left[\sum_{i=1}^{N_P}\left[\sum_{k=1}^{K}\frac{I(x_{ik})}{K}\right]\right]/N_P\right\}$$

$$= \left(\frac{1}{N}\right)\frac{\sum_{i=1}^{N_P}\left[\sum_{k=1}^{K}I(x_{ik})\right]}{K} = \left(\frac{1}{N}\right)\sum_{i=1}^{N_P}c_i \tag{24}$$

where c_i refers to the proportion of assets that individual i does not have.

In other words, M_0 is equal to the ratio of the total number of assets that the individuals (households) classified as poor do not have, over the maximal number (NK) of assets that the total population could be deprived of.

Alkire and Foster (2019) then generalized their approach and defined an index

$$M_0 = \frac{1}{N}\sum_{i=1}^{N}c_i^{\gamma}(k) \ for \ \gamma \geq 0 \tag{25}$$

where $c_i^{\gamma}(k) = c_i^{\gamma}$ if individual i is multidimensionally poor $(c_i \geq k)$ and $c_i^{\gamma}(k) = 0$ otherwise.

Alternative Counting Approaches

The approach of Alkire and Foster (2011) is not the only way of deriving a measure of poverty when only binary or ordinal variables are available. Atkinson (2003) gave a nice introduction to the counting approach and stressed that it is an important topic because in many cases the data available on the various dimensions of poverty are binary variables.

Let c_i be defined as before. Dhongde et al. (2016) called c_i the "nominal deprivation" of individual i while they defined the "real deprivation" of individual i as $r_i = g(c_i)$.

The extent r of "real deprivation" in the population is then expressed as

$$r = \left(\frac{1}{N}\right)\sum_{i=1}^{N}g(c_i) \tag{26}$$

Yalonetzky (2012), and Silber and Yalonetzky (2013) extended expression (26) to obtain, as special case, the approach of Alkire and Foster (2011). Calling RD_i the "real deprivation" of individual (household) i, as defined by Silber and Yalonetzky (2013), they defined RD_i as

$$RD_i = \psi_i r_i = \psi_i g(c_i) \tag{27}$$

In (29) ψ_i refers to some poverty identification function for individual i. One possibility, as implicitly suggested by Alkire and Foster (2011), is to assume that $\psi_i = 1$ if c_i, the extent of "nominal deprivation" (that is, the weighted number of assets that individual or household i does not have), is higher than or equal to $k_{critical}$, the threshold defined previously, and that ψ_i will be equal to 0 otherwise.

Several different functions ψ_i and r_i have been proposed in the literature (see Silber and Yalonetzky, 2013, for illustrations). One interesting suggestion is that of Rippin (2012), who assumed that $\psi_i = 1$ and $r_i = c_i^{1+\gamma}$ so that

$$RD_i^{Rippin} = \frac{1}{N} \sum_{i=1}^{N} c_i^{\gamma+1}. \tag{28}$$

Note that the measure proposed by Rippin (2012) takes into account the degree of inequality, between the individuals (households) classified as poor, in the number of assets they do not have, while the measure introduced by Alkire and Foster (2011) ignores such an inequality.

5.4 Inequality-Sensitive and Additive Achievement Measures Based on Ordinal data

In an important paper Atkinson (1970) defined the concept of "equally distributed equivalent income,"[23] which is the level of income that, if received by every individual, would put society at a level of welfare identical to the actual level of welfare. Apouey, Silber, and Xu (2020) attempted to obtain a somewhat similar result for the case where only ordinal variables are available. They derived axiomatically new classes of measures of the level of achievement in a population when the achievement variable is ordinal. With K durables, there are $(K+1)$ possible durables ownership categories so that in such a case the social achievement index they proposed would be written as

$$h(s) = \frac{1}{N} \sum_{k=1}^{K} p_k(s) \frac{1 - \alpha^{(K+1)-k}}{1 - \alpha^{(K+1)-1}} = \frac{1}{N} \sum_{k=1}^{K} p_k(s) \frac{1 - \alpha^{(K+1)-k}}{1 - \alpha^K} \tag{29}$$

with $0 < \alpha < 1$ and where s refers to the achievements, ranked by decreasing levels, $(K+1)$ to the number of achievement categories (since there are K durable goods), $p_k(s)$ to the number of individuals with achievement level k, and N to the total number of individuals.[24]

When the parameter α tends towards 1, the social achievement index will be expressed as

---

[23] Most of the results presented in Atkinson (1970) appear, in fact, in Kolm (1969), but Atkinson was not aware of this. Kolm did not use the expression "equally distributed equivalent income." He labeled this concept the "equal equivalent income."

[24] See Apouey, Silber, and Xu (2018) for the list of desirable properties of such an index and for its axiomatic derivation.

$$h(s) = \frac{1}{N} \sum_{k=1}^{K} p_k(s) \frac{(K+1) - k}{K} \tag{30}$$

In such a case it can be shown that

$$h(s) = \frac{1}{(K-1)} \sum_{k=1}^{K-1} F_k(s) \tag{31}$$

where $F_k(s) = \sum_{j=1}^{k} \left(\frac{p_j(s)}{n} \right)$, that is, $F_k(s)$ is the cumulative relative frequency of the various achievement categories.

5.5 Empirical Illustrations

This empirical illustration is based on data from the 2019 Eurobarometer survey and covers thirty-five countries, whose list appears in Table 8. It includes the following durable goods or services: Regular phone (1), Mobile phone (2), Television (3), DVD (4), CD player (5), Computer (6), Laptop (7), Tablet (8), Smartphone (9), Connection to Internet (10), Car (11), and House that has already been paid for (12).

Measuring Ordinal Inequality

In Table 8 we used the order of acquisition derived from the approach of Paroush and computed for each country five different ordinal inequality indices: those introduced respectively by Abul Naga and Yalcin (2008), Apouey (2007) and Lv et al. (2015), and one of the indices proposed by Reardon (2009). The same indices appear in Table 9, which is derived from the orders of acquisition obtained when using Item Response Theory. ·

In Table 8 we observe that inequality, whatever index is selected, is highest in Hungary and Slovakia and lowest in the Netherlands and then in Denmark. If we derive the indices from the order of acquisition obtained when using Item Response Theory, we observe in Table 9 that here also Hungary has the highest and the Netherlands the lowest level of ordinal inequality, whatever index is used. Table 10 gives the correlations between the different inequality indices. The numbers above the diagonal are derived from the Paroush approach and those below the diagonal from Item Response Theory. These correlations are always higher than 0.9. In Table 11 we present the correlations between the inequality indices derived from the approach of Paroush and those obtained when applying Item Response Theory. It appears that these correlations are always higher than 0.75, often higher than 0.8 and even 0.9, so that it does not really matter whether

Table 8 Ordinal Inequality Indices computed using the Paroush approach

Country	Abul Naga & Yalcin	Apouey ($\alpha = 0.5$)	Lv et al. LWX_1	Lv et al. $LWX2$ ($\alpha = 0.8$)	Reardon3
France	0.396	0.267	0.541	0.170	0.686
Belgium	0.383	0.256	0.509	0.150	0.626
Netherlands	0.134	0.079	0.206	0.072	0.324
West Germany	0.314	0.196	0.458	0.149	0.616
Italy	0.453	0.296	0.611	0.183	0.733
Luxembourg	0.266	0.155	0.413	0.141	0.598
Denmark	0.221	0.142	0.310	0.100	0.457
Ireland	0.294	0.190	0.422	0.135	0.599
United Kingdom	0.323	0.201	0.462	0.142	0.615
Greece	0.411	0.279	0.543	0.159	0.643
Spain	0.364	0.234	0.510	0.154	0.653
Portugal	0.401	0.241	0.588	0.176	0.726
East Germany	0.464	0.301	0.632	0.195	0.758
Finland	0.254	0.158	0.374	0.120	0.529
Sweden	0.272	0.179	0.385	0.117	0.517
Austria	0.252	0.160	0.361	0.113	0.518
Cyprus Republic	0.427	0.289	0.552	0.158	0.642
Czech Republic	0.463	0.309	0.611	0.184	0.718
Estonia	0.453	0.309	0.592	0.176	0.711
Hungary	0.511	0.335	0.674	0.206	0.778
Latvia	0.484	0.335	0.619	0.184	0.730
Lithuania	0.436	0.309	0.551	0.161	0.678
Malta	0.485	0.330	0.619	0.182	0.696
Poland	0.448	0.316	0.577	0.169	0.688
Slovakia	0.499	0.335	0.660	0.203	0.784
Slovenia	0.403	0.272	0.533	0.159	0.657
Bulgaria	0.394	0.285	0.501	0.145	0.639
Romania	0.376	0.260	0.487	0.141	0.613
Turkey	0.295	0.193	0.425	0.132	0.570
Croatia	0.364	0.227	0.520	0.154	0.643
Cyprus (TCC)	0.348	0.232	0.462	0.133	0.540
North Macedonia	0.416	0.275	0.564	0.165	0.683
Montenegro	0.293	0.186	0.426	0.127	0.573
Serbia	0.354	0.217	0.506	0.147	0.619
Albania	0.281	0.172	0.420	0.128	0.604

Notes: It can be shown that the index LWX_1 is identical to the index Reardon2 and that the index of Abul Naga and Yalcin is identical to the index Reardon4.

The index Reardon1 could not be computed because there were many zeros in the data matrix, and hence the logarithmic function which appears in the formulation of the index Reardon1 could not be used.

Table 9 Ordinal Inequality Indices computed using Item Response Theory

Country	Abul Naga & Yalcin	Apouey ($\alpha = 0.5$)	Lv et al. LWX_1	Lv et al. $LWX2$ ($\alpha = 0.8$)	Reardon3
France	0.340	0.215	0.485	0.153	0.643
Belgium	0.367	0.239	0.497	0.148	0.621
Netherlands	0.128	0.074	0.201	0.071	0.322
West Germany	0.288	0.174	0.427	0.141	0.592
Italy	0.498	0.339	0.648	0.197	0.758
Luxembourg	0.226	0.130	0.360	0.134	0.566
Denmark	0.218	0.139	0.306	0.099	0.452
Ireland	0.299	0.186	0.439	0.139	0.617
United Kingdom	0.282	0.172	0.418	0.136	0.593
Greece	0.275	0.179	0.388	0.123	0.540
Spain	0.390	0.245	0.555	0.166	0.687
Portugal	0.369	0.218	0.560	0.170	0.713
East Germany	0.489	0.320	0.655	0.201	0.777
Finland	0.247	0.157	0.358	0.116	0.515
Sweden	0.220	0.134	0.326	0.103	0.464
Austria	0.250	0.153	0.365	0.116	0.525
Cyprus Republic	0.304	0.185	0.444	0.133	0.579
Czech Republic	0.485	0.335	0.629	0.190	0.731
Estonia	0.440	0.314	0.557	0.165	0.690
Hungary	0.465	0.297	0.649	0.202	0.774
Latvia	0.451	0.282	0.628	0.190	0.744
Lithuania	0.404	0.285	0.508	0.145	0.640
Malta	0.405	0.280	0.526	0.150	0.609
Poland	0.382	0.237	0.552	0.163	0.679
Slovakia	0.504	0.339	0.666	0.205	0.791
Slovenia	0.387	0.261	0.508	0.150	0.636
Bulgaria	0.359	0.261	0.451	0.130	0.585
Romania	0.332	0.228	0.430	0.124	0.552
Turkey	0.267	0.169	0.392	0.125	0.548
Croatia	0.373	0.231	0.533	0.158	0.652
Cyprus (TCC)*	0.350	0.235	0.465	0.134	0.542
North Macedonia	0.391	0.252	0.549	0.163	0.682
Montenegro	0.293	0.186	0.426	0.127	0.573
Serbia	0.389	0.245	0.539	0.156	0.641
Albania	0.311	0.194	0.453	0.136	0.626

Notes: It can be shown that the index LWX_1 is identical to the index Reardon2 and that the index of Abul Naga and Yalcin is identical to the index Reardon4.

The index Reardon1 could not be computed because there were many zeros in the data matrix, and hence the logarithmic function which appears in the formulation of the index Reardon1 could not be used.

Table 10 Correlations between the ordinal inequality indices (above
the diagonal, using the the Paroush approach; below the diagonal using Item
Response Theory)

	Abul Naga & Yalcin	Apouey $(\alpha = 0.5)$	Lv et al. LWX_1	Lv et al. $LWX2$	Reardon3
Abul Naga & Yalcin	1.000	0.989	0.984	0.954	0.931
Apouey $(\alpha = 0.5)$	0.985	1.000	0.949	0.908	0.884
Lv et al. LWX_1	0.979	0.932	1.000	0.985	0.970
Lv et al. $LWX2$	0.938	0.877	0.979	1.000	0.980
Reardon3	0.926	0.865	0.972	0.981	1.000

Table 11 Correlations between indices derived from the Paroush approach
and those derived from Item Response Theory

	Abul Naga & Yalcin (Paroush)	Apouey $(\alpha = 0.5)$ (Paroush)	Lv et al. LWX_1 (Paroush)	Lv et al. $LWX2$ $(\alpha = 0.8)$ (Paroush)	Reardon3 (Paroush)
Abul Naga & Yalcin (IRT)	0.901	0.867	0.913	0.899	0.893
Apouey $(\alpha = 0.5)$ (IRT)	0.889	0.872	0.882	0.859	0.852
Lv et al. LWX_1 (IRT)	0.885	0.832	0.922	0.920	0.921
Lv et al. $LWX2$ $(\alpha = 0.8)$ (IRT)	0.844	0.777	0.899	0.929	0.923
Reardon3 (IRT)	0.838	0.774	0.898	0.919	0.947

we base our analysis of ordinal inequality on the order of acquisition derived from the approach of Paroush or from Item Response Theory.

Computing Multidimensional Poverty Indices

In Table 12, based on the approach of Paroush, and Table 13, derived from Item Response Theory, we computed several multidimensional poverty indices that can be used when dealing with ordinal variables. The three first indices are those proposed by Alkire and Foster (2011) that were defined previously, namely the headcount ratio H, the average deprivation share A, and the adjusted headcount ratio M_0. As mentioned before, Alkire and Foster (2019) generalized their index and defined an index M_0^γ. The result obtained when their parameter γ is equal to 2 is given in the fifth column of Tables 12 and 13. Finally in the last column of these two tables we computed the index introduced by Rippin (2010, 2012) when her parameter γ is equal to 1. In Table 12 it appears that multidimensional poverty is highest in Turkey when using Alkire and Foster's index M_0 or its generalization M_0^2, and in Slovakia when using Rippin's index. But it is always lowest in the Netherlands. When applying Item Response Theory, we observe in Table 13 that multidimensional poverty is again highest in Turkey when using the index M_0 or its generalization M_0^2 and in Romania when using Rippin's index. But multidimensional poverty is always lowest in the Netherlands. Table 14 gives the correlations between the various poverty indices, the numbers above the diagonal being derived from the Paroush approach and those below from Item Response Theory. The numbers on the diagonal give the correlation, for each index, between the Paroush approach and Item Response Theory.

Finally in Table 15 we computed the achievement index recently proposed by Apouey et al. (2020). As mentioned previously, when the parameter α is equal to 0.999, this achievement index does not take account of the extent of inequality between the individual achievements while inequality is also taken account of when, for example, the parameter α is equal to 0.5. It appears that, whether we use the Paroush approach or Item Response Theory, the achievement index is highest in the Netherlands, whether we take inequality into account or not. When ignoring inequality, the achievement index is highest in the Netherlands and lowest in Slovakia when $\alpha = 0.5$ and highest in Albania and lowest in Turkey when $\alpha = 0.999$.

In Table 16 we computed the correlations between these indices, and they are always higher than 0.835.

Table 12 Multidimensional poverty indices, using the Paroush approach

Country	H	A	M_0	Generalized Alkire & Foster index $M_0^{\gamma=2}$	Rippin index with $\gamma = 1$
France	0.270	0.606	0.163	0.108	0.077
Belgium	0.300	0.551	0.165	0.095	0.058
Netherlands	0.025	0.462	0.012	0.006	0.003
West Germany	0.168	0.629	0.106	0.072	0.053
Italy	0.457	0.599	0.274	0.175	0.119
Luxembourg	0.148	0.615	0.091	0.062	0.047
Denmark	0.301	0.460	0.138	0.067	0.034
Ireland	0.219	0.561	0.123	0.077	0.053
United Kingdom	0.229	0.555	0.127	0.076	0.050
Greece	0.309	0.605	0.187	0.115	0.073
Spain	0.341	0.548	0.187	0.112	0.074
Portugal	0.600	0.607	0.364	0.246	0.182
East Germany	0.417	0.683	0.285	0.208	0.160
Finland	0.179	0.575	0.103	0.065	0.044
Sweden	0.243	0.503	0.122	0.064	0.035
Austria	0.197	0.511	0.101	0.055	0.033
Cyprus Republic	0.432	0.610	0.263	0.163	0.103
Czech Republic	0.444	0.643	0.285	0.196	0.143
Estonia	0.713	0.645	0.459	0.313	0.222
Hungary	0.565	0.666	0.376	0.268	0.200
Latvia	0.680	0.686	0.467	0.342	0.264
Lithuania	0.736	0.664	0.489	0.342	0.249
Malta	0.403	0.625	0.252	0.161	0.106
Poland	0.763	0.645	0.492	0.345	0.257
Slovakia	0.705	0.700	0.494	0.367	0.286
Slovenia	0.309	0.552	0.170	0.102	0.066
Bulgaria	0.789	0.636	0.502	0.342	0.247
Romania	0.765	0.668	0.511	0.355	0.255
Turkey	0.866	0.643	0.557	0.369	0.250
Croatia	0.364	0.551	0.200	0.120	0.078
Cyprus (TCC)*	0.471	0.486	0.229	0.114	0.059
North Macedonia	0.648	0.624	0.404	0.268	0.186
Montenegro	0.528	0.528	0.279	0.159	0.098
Serbia	0.394	0.606	0.239	0.151	0.098
Albania	0.858	0.641	0.549	0.368	0.258

Note: The indices H, A, and M_0 are those introduced by Alkire and Foster(2011). The generalized Alkire and Foster index is discussed in Alkire and Foster (2019). The Rippin approach is discussed in Rippin (2010; 2012).

Table 13 Multidimensional poverty indices, using Item Response Theory

Country	H	A	M_0	Generalized Alkire & Foster index $M_0^{\gamma=2}$	Rippin index with $\gamma = 1$
France	0.231	0.588	0.136	0.087	0.062
Belgium	0.282	0.543	0.153	0.088	0.054
Netherlands	0.026	0.462	0.012	0.006	0.003
West Germany	0.143	0.621	0.089	0.061	0.046
Italy	0.424	0.641	0.271	0.183	0.129
Luxembourg	0.101	0.705	0.071	0.055	0.046
Denmark	0.296	0.457	0.135	0.065	0.033
Ireland	0.252	0.565	0.142	0.089	0.062
United Kingdom	0.107	0.689	0.074	0.054	0.042
Greece	0.100	0.625	0.063	0.042	0.029
Spain	0.420	0.579	0.243	0.152	0.103
Portugal	0.603	0.588	0.355	0.236	0.175
East Germany	0.435	0.738	0.321	0.246	0.196
Finland	0.137	0.604	0.083	0.054	0.038
Sweden	0.135	0.522	0.070	0.038	0.021
Austria	0.176	0.515	0.091	0.051	0.032
Cyprus Republic	0.167	0.606	0.101	0.064	0.043
Czech Republic	0.483	0.643	0.310	0.213	0.156
Estonia	0.754	0.669	0.505	0.357	0.262
Hungary	0.450	0.627	0.282	0.196	0.148
Latvia	0.602	0.657	0.396	0.287	0.223
Lithuania	0.765	0.673	0.515	0.367	0.272
Malta	0.295	0.573	0.169	0.099	0.059
Poland	0.773	0.598	0.462	0.308	0.226
Slovakia	0.717	0.686	0.492	0.360	0.277
Slovenia	0.302	0.526	0.159	0.091	0.057
Bulgaria	0.840	0.626	0.526	0.353	0.251
Romania	0.809	0.668	0.540	0.376	0.269
Turkey	0.875	0.660	0.577	0.389	0.267
Croatia	0.379	0.552	0.209	0.126	0.082
Cyprus (TCC)*	0.478	0.489	0.234	0.117	0.061
North Macedonia	0.526	0.595	0.313	0.199	0.135
Montenegro	0.528	0.528	0.279	0.159	0.098
Serbia	0.377	0.640	0.242	0.158	0.106
Albania	0.813	0.640	0.520	0.349	0.245

Note: The indices H, A, and M_0 are those introduced by Alkire and Foster(2011). The generalized Alkire and Foster index is discussed in Alkire and Foster (2019). The Rippin approach is discussed in Rippin (2010, 2012).

Table 14 Correlations between various multidimensional poverty indices

	H	A	M_0	Generalized Alkire & Foster index $M_0^{\gamma=2}$	Rippin index with $\gamma = 1$
H	0.959	0.570	0.946	0.929	0.909
A	0.417	0.854	0.498	0.549	0.579
M_0	0.954	0.651	0.959	0.952	0.940
Generalized Alkire & Foster index $M_0^{\gamma=2}$	0.936	0.708	0.955	0.960	0.955
Rippin with $\gamma = 1$	0.914	0.748	0.944	0.959	0.963

Note: The numbers above the diagonal are derived from the Paroush approach; those below the diagonal are derived from Item Response Theory.

5.6 Concluding Comments

In this section we showed how information on the order of acquisition of durable goods and assets may be used to draw conclusions concerning the extent of inequality, poverty, and even welfare, in different countries. To derive such information, we used results that appeared relatively recently in the literature focusing on the measurement of inequality, poverty, and achievement when only ordinal variables are available. This is evidently the case of data giving the order of acquisition of durable goods and assets. The empirical illustration we presented, which was also based on the 2019 Eurobarometer Survey, confirmed the usefulness of these ordinal indices.

6 On the Order of Curtailment of Expenditures

6.1 Introduction

The last section of this book is devoted not to the order of acquisition of durable goods that is assumed to give a picture of the extent of wealth of an individual or household but rather to the order of curtailment of expenditures which is supposed to describe what happens when individuals or households start facing financial difficulties. Section 6.2 reviews the rather scant literature on this topic, while Section 6.3 gives an empirical illustration based on the 2013 Social Survey in Israel. This is the last Israeli social survey where quite a large number of questions on the curtailing of expenditures were available. To derive the order of curtailment of expenditures we adapt the Paroush approach as well as Item

Table 15 Apouey et al. (2020) achievement index using the Paroush approach and Item Response Theory

Country	Paroush approach with $\alpha = 0.5$	Paroush approach with $\alpha = 0.999$	Item Response Theory with $\alpha = 0.5$	Item Response Theory with $\alpha = 0.999$	Per capita GDP at PPP in 2019
France	0.969	0.753	0.974	0.769	49,435
Belgium	0.985	0.755	0.985	0.768	54,545
Netherlands	0.998	0.870	0.998	0.874	59,687
West Germany	0.978	0.807	0.978	0.825	not available
Italy	0.959	0.651	0.954	0.657	44,197
Luxembourg	0.972	0.840	0.970	0.866	1,21,293
Denmark	0.991	0.709	0.992	0.712	59,830
Ireland	0.974	0.751	0.971	0.727	88,241
United Kingdom	0.981	0.777	0.978	0.811	48,710
Greece	0.983	0.724	0.990	0.821	31,399
Spain	0.973	0.708	0.966	0.657	42,214
Portugal	0.919	0.557	0.916	0.562	36,471
East Germany	0.923	0.608	0.902	0.561	not available
Finland	0.985	0.763	0.986	0.772	51,324
Sweden	0.992	0.761	0.995	0.796	55,815
Austria	0.989	0.731	0.988	0.757	59,111
Cyprus Republic	0.978	0.642	0.987	0.760	41,254
Czech Republic	0.943	0.624	0.939	0.612	42,576
Estonia	0.930	0.497	0.913	0.450	38,811

Table 15 (cont.)

Country	Paroush approach with $\alpha = 0.5$	Paroush approach with $\alpha = 0.999$	Item Response Theory with $\alpha = 0.5$	Item Response Theory with $\alpha = 0.999$	Per capita GDP at PPP in 2019
Hungary	0.924	0.558	0.933	0.636	33,979
Latvia	0.886	0.466	0.890	0.520	32,204
Lithuania	0.918	0.458	0.906	0.428	38,214
Malta	0.974	0.678	0.988	0.748	45,652
Poland	0.896	0.461	0.899	0.495	34,218
Slovakia	0.865	0.459	0.867	0.471	34,178
Slovenia	0.980	0.754	0.981	0.751	40,657
Bulgaria	0.909	0.446	0.909	0.430	24,561
Romania	0.922	0.434	0.918	0.407	32,297
Turkey	0.936	0.426	0.931	0.406	27,875
Croatia	0.976	0.691	0.975	0.688	29,973
Cyprus (TCC)*	0.991	0.698	0.991	0.694	not available
North Macedonia	0.943	0.526	0.955	0.593	17,815
Montenegro	0.974	0.614	0.974	0.614	not available
Serbia	0.976	0.630	0.974	0.631	18,989
Albania	0.905	0.420	0.908	0.437	14,495

Note: When using the Paroush approach, the correlation between the Apouey et al. index and the per capita GDP in 2019 is equal to 0.667 when $\alpha = 0.999$ and to 0.457 when $\alpha = 0.5$. The corresponding correlations when using Item Response Theory are 0.603 and 0.421.

Table 16 Correlations between the achievement indices of Apouey et al. (2020)

	Achievement Index with $\alpha = 0.5$ (Paroush)	Achievement index with $\alpha = 0.999$ (Paroush)
Achievement index with $\alpha = 0.5$ (IRT)	0.982	0.850
Achievement index with $\alpha = 0.999$ (IRT)	0.835	0.963

Note: The number above the diagonal refers to results based on the Paroush approach. The number below the diagonal refers to those derived from Item Response Theory. The numbers on the diagonal refer to correlations between results based on the Paroush approach and those derived from Item Response Theory.

Response Theory to this issue. The section ends with the presentation of results of a Logit regression, where we examine the determinants of the extent of the cutback of expenditures.

6.2 A Short Review of the Literature on the Order of Curtailment of Expenditures

In Section 2 we cited Dupuit (1844), who almost two centuries ago wrote that if "the income of the individual in question decreases progressively . . .," "he is obliged to gradually eliminate the articles which he considers the least indispensable." This idea of order of curtailment of expenditures has been examined in several relatively recent studies. The discovery of this order of curtailment uses the same algorithm as that implemented when trying to detect the order of acquisition of durable goods. In other words what is analyzed here is the reverse situation: one wishes to find out in which order individuals or households curtail their expenditures when they face a serious decrease in their income or wealth. In what follows we review a few studies that analyzed the order of curtailment of expenditures.

Deutsch, Lazar, and Silber (2013) used the 2003 Israeli Social Survey that provided quite a detailed information on the consumption of various health- and non-health-related goods and services. The authors, however, warned us to be careful in drawing conclusion after such an analysis. They stress that deprivation is a latent variable and that they analyzed data from a cross-section. Since families face different types of hardship, the order of curtailment is likely to depend on the hardship they cope with. A household with young children and insufficient income is more likely to curtail certain medical expenses than food, while a household with two elderly persons will probably prefer to cut food rather than prescription medications. These caveats have therefore to be kept in mind before drawing clear-cut conclusions. The questions of the Social Survey that the authors considered are the following ones:

- Did the individual forgo dental work in the past twelve months because he/she could not afford it?
- Did the individual forgo buying prescription drugs in the past twelve months because he/she could not afford it?
- Did the individual forgo receiving any medical treatment (other than dental work or prescription drugs) in the past twelve months because he/she could not afford it?
- Is the reason the individual does not have additional health insurance coverage because he/she cannot afford it?
- In the past twelve months, did the individual forgo adequately heating in his/her dwelling because he/she could not afford it?
- In the past twelve months, did the individual forgo buying clothing or shoes because he/she could not afford it?
- In the past twelve months, was the electricity or phone service disconnected because the individual could not afford to pay your bills?
- In the past twelve months, did the individual sometimes not eat because he/she did not have enough money?

Given the relatively high degree of nonresponse on some of the questions, the authors made several investigations, analyzing each time a somewhat different set of expenditures. When they excluded from their analysis the question relative to a medical treatment other than dental work or prescription drugs and that relative to an additional health insurance, they concluded that the order of curtailment of expenditures with the highest proximity index was as follows: Clothing or Shoes, Dental Work, Heating or Cooling, Food, Prescription Drugs, and Electricity or Phone interruption. Other orders of curtailment are presented in the paper by Deutsch, Lazar, and Silber (2013).

In the second stage of their analysis, the authors estimated an ordered logit regression for each of the order of curtailment considered. As explanatory variables they included the age of the individual and its square, the gender of the individual, the household size, the highest diploma received by the individual, the area of residence, marital status, religion, the income level, the country of birth of the individual, as well as that of his/her father, and a dummy variable equal to 1 when young children were present. The results of these regression are given in the paper of Deutsch, Lazar and Silber (2013).

The same type of analysis was undertaken by Deutsch et al. (2015). The focus of their study was on material deprivation in Europe. To derive what they called the deprivation sequence, the authors used two approaches, the algorithm suggested by Paroush (1963, 1965, 1973) and Item Response Theory. Our focus here on the approach of Paroush. The main goal of the authors was to rank the thirteen material deprivation items proposed by Guio et al. (2012) and compare this ranking across the European Union (EU). This list of thirteen items includes first "Adult items," that is, items collected among individuals that were adult. This adult deprivation information was then assigned to all household members if at least half the adults for which the information is available lacked and could not afford

- to replace worn-out clothes by some new (not second-hand) ones
- two pairs of properly fitting shoes, including a pair of all-weather shoes
- to spend a small amount of money each week on oneself without having to consult anyone
- to get together with friends/family for a drink/meal at least monthly
- to have regular leisure activities

In addition, there were "Household items," which were collected at the household level. This household deprivation information was then assigned to all household members when, according to the household head, the household lacked and could not afford

- to replace worn-out furniture (but would like to have new furniture)
- a meal with meat, chicken, fish or vegetarian equivalent every second day
- to face unexpected expenses
- to keep home adequately warm
- one-week annual holiday away from home
- to avoid arrears (mortgage or rent, utility bills or purchase instalments)
- a car/van for private use (but would like to have one)
- a computer and an Internet connection (but would like to have one)

For the EU as a whole the order of curtailment was as follows: (1) Holidays, (2) unexpected expenses, (3) furniture, (4) leisure, (5) pocket money, (6) drink/meal out, (7) clothes, (8) meat/chicken/fish, (9) home warm, (10) car, (11) arrears, (12) computer/Internet, (13) shoes.

The authors also derived the order of curtailment specific to each country as well as that concerning the following population subgroups: households with two adults or more, with and without children, single households, and single households older or younger than sixty-five. It appears that the rank correlations between the countries are quite high (in many cases well above 0.5). As far as within-country variations are concerned, the authors concluded that the Deprivation Sequence of the country, as a whole, is very similar to that of the various population subgroups considered.

In another study Deutsch, Silber, and Wan (2017) analyzed data on the curtailment of expenditures in three South Caucasian States, namely Azerbaijan, Armenia, and Georgia. Their database was the so-called Caucasus Barometer, and they analyzed the 2009 and 2013 surveys. They considered seven components of the households' expenditures: bread; milk; meat, that is, poultry, beef, or fish; vegetables; potatoes; electricity; and transportation. The authors concluded that in both years, there was a high correlation between these countries in the order of curtailment of consumption expenditures. For Armenia, for example, in 2009, the order of curtailment was as follows: electricity, transportation, meat (i.e. beef, poultry, or fish), milk, vegetables, bread, and potatoes.

6.3 A New Illustration of the Order of Curtailment of Expenditures

Here we use the data from the 2013 Israel Social Survey, which included many questions on the curtailment of expenditures when the financial situation of a household deteriorates. This kind of questions does not appear every year in the social survey. The most recent survey which included these questions was that of 2013. Here is the list of questions we included in our analysis:

1 In the last twelve months, have you given up **food**, due to financial difficulties?

2 In the last twelve months, have you given up **a hot meal at least once every two days**, due to financial difficulties?

3 In the last twelve months, have you given up on **inviting family members or friends over for a meal**, because of financial difficulties?

4 In the last twelve months, have you given up **buying clothes or shoes** because of financial difficulties?

5 In the past twelve months, have you given up **unexpected expenses such as a gift for a family event or car repair**, because of financial difficulties?

6 In the last twelve months, have you given up **a hobby or leisure activity**, due to financial difficulties?

7 In the last twelve months, have you given up on **heating or cooling your home adequately**, due to financial difficulties?

8 In the last twelve months, have you given up on **repairing defects in your apartment such as dampness in the apartment, a leaking roof**, because of financial difficulties?

9 In the last twelve months, have you given up on **replacing worn or broken furniture** in your home, due to financial difficulties?

10 In the last twelve months, have you given up on **replacing broken electronics or electrical appliances**, because of financial difficulties?

11 In the last twelve months, have you given up on **dental care**, due to financial difficulties?

12 In the last twelve months, have you given up **medical treatment**, due to financial difficulties?

13 In the last twelve months, have you given up **prescription drugs** because of financial difficulties?

In Table 17 we present the order of curtailment obtained using first the Paroush approach, then Item Response Theory. The first line of the table refers to the thirteen questions that have just been mentioned, while the second line gives the rank of each type of curtailment. The rankings derived from the two approaches are very similar. In fact the coefficient of rank correlation between these two rankings is equal to 0.98.

A close look at the orders of curtailing derived with the two approaches shows that in both cases the two first expenditures that are curtailed are "buying clothes or shoes" and then "giving up a hobby or a leisure activity." In both approaches the next five types of expenditures curtailed are unexpected expenses such as a gift for a family event or car repair, heating or cooling your home adequately, replacing worn or broken furniture, replacing broken electronics or electrical appliances, and dental care. The ordering of these five types of expenditures is slightly different when using the Paroush approach and Item Response Theory. Finally note that the last four types of expenditures that are curtailed are food, a hot meal at least once every two days, medical treatment, and prescription drugs. The Paroush approach gives medical treatment as last expenditure to be cut, while Item Response Theory gives prescription drugs.

In Table 18 we present the distribution of the number of curtailed expenditures obtained in the most common path of curtailment which was derived when using respectively the Paroush approach and Item Response Theory. One line gives the relative frequencies of the number of expenditures curtailed, the other the cumulative frequencies. The coefficient of correlation between the relative frequencies obtained respectively with the Paroush approach and Item Response Theory turns out to be equal to 0.999.

Note that both approaches show that 65 percent of the households do not curtail any expenditure. This could be interpreted as indicating that 35 percent

Table 17 Order of curtailing expenditures and Reproducibility Index

The Paroush approach

	1	2	3	4	5	6	7	8	9	10	11	12	13	Reproducibility Index
Expenditure curtailed (code)	1	2	3	4	5	6	7	8	9	10	11	12	13	
Rank of expenditure curtailed	4	6	5	7	9	10	11	8	3	1	2	13	12	0.9083

Item Response Theory

	1	2	3	4	5	6	7	8	9	10	11	12	13	Number of observations
Expenditure curtailed (code)	1	2	3	4	5	6	7	8	9	10	11	12	13	
Rank of expenditure curtailed	4	6	7	5	9	11	10	3	8	1	2	12	13	2416

Table 18 Distribution of the number of curtailed expenditures in the most common path

The Paroush approach

Number of expenditures curtailed	0	1	2	3	4	5	6	7	8	9	10	11	12	13
Relative frequency	65.3	2.8	1.5	2.6	0.4	0.3	1.4	1.1	1.5	3.6	1.8	6.7	3.2	7.8
Cumulative relative frequency	65.3	68.1	69.6	72.2	72.7	73.0	74.4	75.5	77.1	80.7	82.4	89.1	92.2	100

Item Response Theory

Number of expenditures curtailed	0	1	2	3	4	5	6	7	8	9	10	11	12	13
Relative frequency	67.8	2.9	1.6	1.0	0.5	0.3	0.3	1.1	1.9	3.7	1.8	6.9	2.5	8.0
Cumulative relative frequency	67.4	70.3	71.9	72.9	73.4	73.7	74.0	75.2	77.1	80.8	82.6	89.5	92.0	100

of the households are poor in some sense; that is, these are households that cut at least one type of expenditures. One could, however, define a different "poverty line" and decide, for example, that to be considered as poor, one should curtail more than half the number of types of expenditures. In such a case that would imply that at least seven types of expenditures have been curtailed and then both approaches show that around 23 percent of the households would be considered as poor.

In the next stage of our analysis, we computed a measure of the extent of the inequality in the distribution of the number of expenditures curtailed. Here we need to apply inequality indices that have been introduced in recent years for the case where only ordinal variables are available.

As an illustration (see Table 19), we computed one of the indices introduced by Reardon[25] (2009), the one which is a combination of equations (15) and (17) in Section 5 and which is hence defined as

$$I_{REARDON} = \frac{1}{K} \sum_{k=0}^{K-1} 4P_k(1 - P_k) \tag{32}$$

where K refers to the number of types of expenditures considered and P_k to the cumulative frequency of the number of expenditures curtailed.[26] This $I_{REARDON}$ index varies between 0 and 1, being equal to 0 when all the individuals curtail the same number of expenditures, and to 1 when half the households do not curtail any expenditure and half of them curtail the maximum number (thirteen here) of expenditures. It turns out that the Reardon index in our empirical illustration is equal to 0.70 when adopting the Paroush approach and to 0.69 when using Item Response Theory.

We then computed the same poverty indices as those described in Section 5, namely the measures H, A, and M_0 introduced by Alkire and Foster (2011), the generalization M_0^2 of the index M_0 that was derived by Alkire and Foster (2019), and the Rippin (2010, 2012) index. For the indices of Alkire and Foster we used three different thresholds: 3, 5, and 8. In other words we assumed that to be considered as poor, one needed to curtail 3, 5, or 8 types of expenditures. The results are given in Table 20. We may observe that here also the results are almost the same whether we adopt the approach of Paroush or use Item Response Theory.

Finally, we computed the achievement index introduced by Apouey et al. (2020), which was defined in equations (29) and (30) in Section 5.4. The results

---

[25] The Reardon index was originally proposed to measure ordinal segregation, but it can evidently be applied to any study involving ordinal variables.

[26] Note that in computing P_k, it does not matter whether the expenditures are ordered by increasing or decreasing number of expenditures curtailed.

Table 19 Ordinal inequality indices

Ordinal inequality index	The Paroush approach	Item Response Theory
Apouey (2007) index with = 0.2	0.126	0.120
Apouey (2007) index with = 0.5	0.282	0.271
Apouey (2007) index with = 0.8	0.405	0.393
Abul Naga and Yalcin index	0.473	0.460
Reardon first index	0.764	0.756
Reardon second index	0.700	0.689
Reardon third index	0.828	0.822
Reardon fourth index	0.473	0.460
Lv et al. (2015) I_{LWX1} index	0.700	0.689
Lv et al. (2015) I_{LWX2} index with $\alpha = 0.2$	0.114	0.120

Table 20 Multidimensional poverty indices, using the approach of Paroush

Poverty index	Using the Paroush approach	Using Item Response Theory
H (threshold = 8)	0.245	0.248
A (threshold = 8)	0.138	0.143
M_0 (threshold = 8)	0.034	0.036
M_0^2 (threshold = 8)	0.008	0.009
Rippin index (threshold = 8)	0.002	0.003
H (threshold = 5)	0.273	0.266
A (threshold = 5)	0.177	0.168
M_0 (threshold = 5)	0.048	0.045
M_0^2 (threshold = 5)	0.016	0.014
Rippin index (threshold = 5)	0.006	0.005
H (threshold = 3)	0.304	0.281
A (threshold = 3)	0.236	0.198
M_0 (threshold = 3)	0.072	0.056
M_0^2 (threshold = 3)	0.034	0.022
Rippin index (threshold = 3)	0.020	0.011

Table 21 Achievement indices

Apouey, Silber, and Xu achievement index	The Paroush approach	Item Response Theory
with parameter $\alpha = 0.2$	0.913	0.912
with parameter $\alpha = 0.5$	0.885	0.885
with parameter $\alpha = 0.999$	0.764	0.770

of this investigation are reported in Table 21. for three different values of the parameter. Note that here again the results based on the order of curtailment derived from the Paroush approach are almost identical to those obtained when using Item Response Theory.

In the last stage of our analysis we estimated ordered logit regressions where the dependent variable was the probability of curtailing $0, 1, \ldots, K$ types of expenditures while the explanatory variables were respectively the gender of the head of the household, his/her age, whether he/she was born (in Israel, in Europe or America or elsewhere), his/her marital status (married, single or other marital status), whether he/she was in good health, whether he/she was Jewish, his/her educational level, whether he/she was working full time and the per capita income of the household. Table 22 presents the results obtained while deriving the order of curtailment of expenditures either from the Paroush approach or when using Item Response Theory.

Ceteris paribus, older heads of household curtail less expenditures, this being also true for heads of household born in Europe or America, although the coefficient of this variable is less significant when using Item Response Theory. We also observe that married and single heads of household curtail less expenditures than divorced or widow(er)s, but this result is significant only when adopting the Paroush approach. Heads of households that are in good health, Jewish, and more educated are also less likely to curtail expenditures, this being true whatever the approach used. Finally, as expected, the higher the per capita income of the household, the lower, ceteris paribus, the number of expenditures that will be curtailed.

6.4 Concluding Comments

In this section we have shown that the same techniques that allow one to derive the order of acquisition of durable goods and assets, namely the Paroush approach and Item Response Theory, may be also applied to obtain information

Table 22 Regression results using the results derived from the approach of Paroush and Item Response Theory

Explanatory variables	Coefficient (Paroush approach)	Standard error (Paroush approach)	Coefficient (Item Response Theory)	Standard error (Item response Theory)
Male	−0.053	0.183	−0.168	0.192
Age	−0.044	0.0077	−0.044	0.008
Born in Israel	−0.205	0.392	−0.281	0.426
Born in Europe or America	−0.971	0.416	−0.702	0.438
Married	−0.692	0.256	−0.217	0.283
Single	−1.163	0.354	−0.652	0.381
Good health	−1.024	0.220	−1.029	0.235
Jew	−0.785	0.250	−0.669	0.249
Education	−0.139	0.038	−0.128	0.039
Working full time	0.214	0.210	0.295	0.225
Per capita income	−0.00040	0.00004	−0.00047	0.00004

Note: Number of observations: 760; Pseudo R-squared for the approach of Paroush: 0.248;
Pseudo R-squared for Item Response Theory: 0.261

on the order of curtailment of expenditures, when an individual or a household starts having financial difficulties. Using the 2013 Israeli Social Survey we found that the order of cutback of expenditures obtained when using the approach of Paroush was very similar to that derived from the application of Item Response Theory. When looking at the determinants of the extent of such cutbacks, we found that age, the place of birth, the marital status, the health, the ethnicity, the level of education, and evidently per capita income had a significant impact on the extent of the curtailment of expenditures.

7 Concluding Comments

For the past twenty years there has been an increasing use of asset indices to measure standards of living, inequality, and poverty, given that in many developing countries reliable data on income or expenditures are not available or not reliable. As stressed by Filmer ad Scott (2012), asset indices are often derived from information on the ownership of goods that tend to be public goods at the household level. On the other hand, especially in developing countries, food is likely to be the main item of consumption expenditures, and food is evidently a private good. In such a case asset indices and per capita consumption cannot be expected to show similar results. It is therefore important to be aware of such a caveat. When making international comparisons of standards of living, the use of purchasing power parity data to determine consumption and income levels and to estimate poverty raises additional issues that were discussed, for example, in Booth (2019), Deaton (2010) and Lustig and Silber (2016). Measuring living standards via data on asset ownership is evidently not without difficulties either, as stressed by Ngo (2018).

Though focusing also on an asset approach to measuring standards of living, this element, following previous work by Paroush (1963) and subsequently by other authors, went one step further and recommended to look at the order of acquisition of assets and durable goods. The idea was that discovering such an order and finding out where individuals (households) are located on such a path allowed one to draw conclusions concerning the standard of living of the different individuals (households).

Such a focus on the order of acquisition of assets and durable goods is in line with a long and quite old tradition in economics that stressed the notion of hierarchical choice. Section 2 reviewed this tradition and gave a short survey of the contributions of the economists that believed in such a hierarchical choice. Particular attention was given to the writings of the French economist René Roy, who is well-known because of the famous "Roy's identity," but who also wrote several important papers on the notion of hierarchical choice.

Section 3 offered first a description of what was labeled the Paroush approach to the derivation of the order of acquisition of durable goods. This section then focused on an alternative way of deriving such an order, one that applied to this issue Item Response Theory, a well-known technique, hitherto mainly used in the field of psychometrics.

Section4 first reviewed previous empirical studies using either the Paroush approach or Item Response Theory. It then presented an empirical illustration based on data from the 2019 Eurobarometer Survey. This survey covered thirty-five countries and this empirical illustration included twelve goods and services. It turned out that the orders of acquisitions derived from the Paroush approach and from Item Response Theory were very similar so that it probably does not matter which technique one selects.

The goal of Section 5 was to use this information on the order of acquisition of durable goods to draw conclusions concerning the extent of inequality, poverty, and welfare in the various countries examined. Given that both the Paroush approach and Item Response Theory focus on ordinal variables, this section started by summarizing studies that explained how inequality, poverty, and welfare could be estimated when working with ordinal variables. The section then presented an empirical illustration, based again on the 2019 Eurobarometer Survey, and derived estimations of the extent of inequality, poverty, and welfare (achievement) in different European countries, using both the Paroush approach and Item Response Theory. It also computed correlation coefficients between the various ordinal inequality indices computed, as well as between the different multidimensional poverty indices that were used.

Section 6 finally took a different perspective to the estimation of the extent of poverty and inequality. The idea was to use data on the curtailment of expenditures that takes place when individuals (households) face financial difficulties. Such data were available in one of the Israeli Social Surveys, the one which was conducted in Israel in 2013, and included information on the curtailment of thirteen types of expenditures by the individuals (households). Here also we applied the Paroush approach as well as Item Response Theory to find out in which order expenditures were cut back. These orders were then used to compute, as in Section 5, multidimensional poverty indices, measures of inequality, and welfare.

It seems therefore that the notion of an order of curtailment of expenditures is as relevant as that of an order of acquisition of durable goods. This book tried to show that both concepts are indeed very useful, to measure not only standards of living but also inequality, poverty, and welfare.

References

Abul Naga, R. H., and T. Yalcin (2008). Inequality Measurement for Ordered Response Health Data. *Journal of Health Economics*, 27(6), 1614–25.

Aitchison, J. and J. A. C. Brown (1954). A Synthesis of Engel Curve Theory. *Review of Economic Studies*, 22(1), 35–46.

Alkire, S. and J. Foster (2011). Counting and Multidimensional Poverty Measurement. *Journal of Public Economics*, 95(7–8), 476–87.

Alkire, S. and J. Foster (2019). The Role of Inequality in Poverty Measurement. OPHI Working Paper No. 126, Oxford: Oxford Poverty and Human Development Initiative.

Allais, M. (1988). La théorie des choix dans l'œuvre de René Roy: Une analyse critique. *Revue d'économie politique*, 98(3), 315–57.

Allison, R. A., and J. Foster (2004). Measuring Health Inequalities Using Qualitative Data. *Journal of Health Economics*, 23, 505–24.

Apouey, B. (2007). Measuring Health Polarization with Self-assessed Health Data. *Health Economics*, 16(9), 875–94.

Apouey, B., J. Silber and Y. Xu (2020). On Inequality-Sensitive and Additive Achievement Measures Based on Ordinal Data. *Review of Income and Wealth*, 66(2), 267–86.

Atkinson, A. B. (1970). On the Measurement of Inequality. *Journal of Economic Theory*, 2(3), 244–63.

Atkinson, A. B. (2003). Multidimensional Deprivation: Contrasting Social Welfare and Counting Approaches. *Journal of Economic Inequality*, 1, 51–65.

Baker, F. B. (2001). The Basics of Item Response Theory. ERIC (Educational Resources Information Center), Clearinghouse on Assessment and Evaluation, Washington, DC: U.S. Department of Education.

Becchio, G. (2014). Social Needs, Social Goods, and Human Associations in the Second Edition of Carl Menger's Principles. *History of Political Economy*, 46(2), 247–64.

Bérenger, V., J. Deutsch and J. Silber (2016). Deriving the Relative Importance of the Various Components of a Household's Standard of Living: The Case of Mexico. *Sobre México: Temas en Economía*, 2(1), 36–61.

Bérenger, V., J. Deutsch and J. Silber (2013). Order of Acquisition of Durable Goods and Multidimensional Poverty Measurement: A Comparative Study of Egypt, Morocco and Turkey. *Economic Modelling*, 35, 881–91.

Booth, A. (2019). Measuring Poverty and Income Distribution in Southeast Asia. *Asian Pacific Economic Literature*, 33(1), 3–20.

Bossert, W., S. Chakravarty and C. D'Ambrosio (2013). Multidimensional Poverty and Material Deprivation with Discrete Data. *Review of Income and Wealth*, 59, 29–43.

Bourdieu, P. (1984). *Distinction: A Social Critique of the Judgment of Taste*. London: Routledge & Kegan Paul.

Brian, É. (2008). Condorcet and Borda in 1784. Misfits and Documents. *Electronic Journal for History of Probability and Statistics*, 4(1).

Cameron, A. C. and D. L. Miller (2014). Robust Inference for Dyadic Data, mimeo, University of California at Davis.

Cappellari, L. and S. P. Jenkins (2007). Summarizing Multiple Deprivation Indicators. In S. P. Jenkins and J. Micklewright (eds.), *Inequality and Poverty: Re-examined*. Oxford: Oxford University Press, pp. 166–84.

Chai, A. and A. Moneta (2010). Retrospectives: Engel Curves. *Journal of Economic Perspectives*, 24(1), 225–40.

Chai, A. and A. Moneta (2012). Back to Engel? Some Evidence for the Hierarchy of Needs. *Journal of Evolutionary Economics*, 22(4), 649–76.

Chai, A., N. Rohde and J. Silber (2015). Measuring the Diversity of Household Spending Patterns. *Journal of Economic Surveys*, 29(3), 423–40.

Chai, A. (2017). Tackling Keynes' Question: A Look Back on 15 Years of Learning to Consume. *Journal of Evolutionary Economics*, 27(2), 251–71.

Chai, A., E. Stepanova and A. Moneta (2022). The Expansion of Global Consumption Diversity and the Rise of Niche Consumption. LEM Papers Series 2022/29, Laboratory of Economics and Management (LEM), Sant'Anna School of Advanced Studies, Pisa, Italy.

Chakravarty, S. and C. D'Ambrosio (2006). The Measurement of Social Exclusion. *Review of Income and Wealth*, 52(3), 377–98.

Clarke, M. (2005). Assessing Well-being Using Hierarchical Needs. In M. McGillivray and M. Clarke (eds.), *Understanding Human Well-being*, Tokyo: United Nations University Press, pp. 217–38.

Clarke, Y. and G. N. Soutar (1982). Consumer Acquisition Patterns for Durable Goods: Australian Evidence. *Journal of Consumer Research*, 8(4), 456–60.

Clements, K. W., Y. Lan, H. Liu and L. Vo (2022). *The ICP, PPP and Household Expenditure Patterns*. Mimeo: University of Western Australia.

Cosmides, L. and J. Tooby (1994). Better than Rational: Evolutionary Psychology and the Invisible Hand. *American Economic Review*, 84(2), 327–32.

Cowell, F. A. and E. Flachaire (2017). Inequality with Ordinal data. *Economica*, 84(334), 290–321.

Crettez, B. (2020). Sur l'analyse microéconomique de la hiérarchie des besoins dans l'économie d'Ancien Régime. *Oeconomia*, 10(4), 711–28.

Deaton, A. (2010). Price Indexes, Inequality and the Measurement of World Poverty. *American Economic Review*, 100(1), 5–34.

Deaton, A. and J. Muellbauer J. (1980). *Economics and Consumer Behavior.* Cambridge: Cambridge University Press.

Debreu, G. (1959). *Theory of Value.* New York: John Wiley.

Deutsch, A., C. Guio, and M. Pomati (2015). Material Deprivation in Europe: Which Expenditures Are Curtailed First? *Social Indicators Research*, 120, 723–40.

Deutsch, J., A. Lazar and J. Silber (2013). Becoming Poor and the Cutback in the Demand for Health Services. *Israel Journal of Health Policy Research*, 2(49), 1–9.

Deutsch, J. and J. Silber (2008). The Order of Acquisition of Durable Goods and the Multidimensional Measurement of Poverty. In N. Kakwani and J. Silber (eds.), *Quantitative Approaches to Multidimensional Poverty Measurement*, New York: Palgrave-Macmillan, pp. 226–43.

Deutsch, J. and J. Silber (2023). The Order of Acquisition of Assets and Deprivation. In J. Silber (ed.), *Research Handbook on Measuring Poverty and Deprivation*, Northampton: Edward Elgar, pp. 511–521

Deutsch, J., J. Silber and G. Wan (2017). Curbing One's Consumption and the Impoverishment Process: The Case of Western Asia. *Research on Economic Inequality*, 25, 137–59.

Deutsch, J., J. Silber, G. Wan and Y. Xu (2020a). Measuring Inequality, Poverty, Growth and Welfare via the Use of Asset Indexes: The Case of Armenia, Azerbaijan and Georgia. *Singapore Economic Review*, 65(Suppl. 1), 7–33.

Deutsch, J., J. Silber, G. Wan and M. Zhao (2020b). Asset Indexes and the Measurement of Poverty, Inequality and Welfare in Southeast Asia. *Journal of Asian Economics*, 70, 1012–20.

Dholakia, R. R. and S. Banerjee (2013). Marketing Household Durables in Emerging Markets: Empirical Evidence from India. *Journal of International Marketing Strategy*, 1(1), 1–14.

Dhongde, S., Y. Li, P.K. Pattanaik and Y. Xu (2016). Binary Data, Hierarchy of Attributes, and Multidimensional Deprivation. *The Journal of Economic Inequality*, 14, 363–78.

Dickes, P. (1983). Modèle de Rasch pour items dichotomiques: Théorie, Technique et application à la mesure de la pauvreté. Nancy: Université de Nancy II, France.

Dickes, P., B. Gailly, P. Hausman and G. Schaber (1984). Les Désavantages de la Pauvreté: Définitions, mesure et réalités en Europe. *Mondes en Développement*, 12(45), 131–90.

Dickes, P. (1989). Pauvreté et Conditions d'Existence: Théories, Modèles et Mesures. Document PSELL No. 8, Walferdange:CEPS/INSTEAD, Luxembourg.

Dickes, P. and A. Fusco (2008). The Rasch Model and Multidimensional Poverty Measurement. In N. Kakwani and J. Silber (eds.), *Quantitative Approaches to Multidimensional Poverty Measurement*. New York: Palgrave Macmillan, pp. 49–62.

Dickinson, J. R. and E. Kirzner (1986). Priority Patterns of Acquisition of Financial Assets. *Journal of the Academy of Marketing Science*, 14(2), 43–9.

Dickson, P. R., R. F. Lusch and W. L. Wilkie (1983). Consumer Acquisition Priorities for Home Appliances: A Replication and Re-evaluation. *Journal of Consumer Research*, 9(4), 432–5.

Drakopoulos, S. A. (1994). Hierarchical Choice in Economics. *Journal of Economic Surveys*, 8, 133–53.

Drakopoulos, S. A. (2004). The Historical Development of Hierarchical Behavior in Economic Thought. *Journal of the History of Economic Thought*, 26(3), 363–78.

Duclos, J., Esteban, J.M., and Ray, D. (2004). Polarization: Concepts, Measurement, Estimation. *Econometrica*, 72(6), 1737–72.

Duesenberry, J. S. (1949). *Income, Saving and the Theory of Consumer Behavior*. Cambridge, MA: Harvard University Press.

Dupuit, A. J. É. J. (1844). De la mesure de l'utilité des travaux publics. *Annales des ponts et chaussées*, Second series, 8. Translated by R. H. Barback as On the measurement of the utility of public works. *International Economic Papers*, 1952, 2, 83–110. Reprinted in: K. J. Arrow and T. Scitovsky, eds., *Readings in Welfare Economics* (Richard D. Irwin, Homewood, IL, 1969), pp. 255–83.

Earl, P. E. and J. Potts (2004). The Market for Preferences. *Cambridge Journal of Economics*, 28(4), 619–33.

Eichner, A. S. (1986). *Toward a New Economics: Essays in Post-Keynesian and Institutionalist Theory*. London: Macmillan, M.E. Sharpe.

Engel, E. (1857). Die Productions- und Consumtionsverhältnisse des Königsreichs Sachsen. *Zeitschrift des Statistischen Bureaus des Königlich Sächsischen Ministeriums des Innern*, 8, 1–54. Reprinted also as appendix to Engel (1895).

Engel, E. (1895). Die Lebenskosten Belgischer Arbeiter-Familien: Fruher Und Jetzt. Kessinger Legacy Reprints.

Esteban, J. and D. Ray (1994). On the Measurement of Polarization. *Econometrica*, 62(4), 819–51.

Falkinger, J. and J. Zweimüller (1996). The Cross-country Engel Curve for Product Diversification. *Structural Change and Economic Dynamics*, 7(1), 79–97.

Farcomeni, A., M. G. Pittau, S. Viviani and R. Zelli (2022). A European Measurement Scale for Material Deprivation. Research Square, Springer Nature. Berlin, Germany.

Filmer, D. and K. Scott (2012). Assessing Assets Indices. *Demography*, 49(1), 359–92.

Fine, B. (1983). The Order of Acquisition of Consumer Durables A Social Choice Theoretic Approach. *Journal of Economic Behavior and Organization*, 4, 239–48.

Fishburn, P. (1974). Lexicographic Orders, Utilities and Decision Rules: A Survey. *Management Science*, 20(11), 1442–71.

Gailly, B. and P. Hausman (1984). Des Désavantages Relatifs à une Mesure Objective de la Pauvreté. In G. Sarpellon (ed.), *Understanding Poverty*, Milan: Franco Angeli, pp. 192–216.

Georgescu-Roegen, N. (1966). *Analytical Economics*. Cambridge: Cambridge University Press.

Goldthorpe, J. K. (1950). An Examination of the Concept of Need. *The Sociological Review*, 42(1), 179–99.

Graham, A. (2022). *Statistics – A Complete Introduction: A Teach Yourself Guide*. McGraw-Hill New York USA.

Guio, A. - C., D. Gordon and E. Marlier (2012). Measuring Material Deprivation in the EU: Indicators for the Whole Population and Child-Specific Indicators. Eurostat Methodologies and working papers, Luxembourg: Office for Official Publications of the European Communities (OPOCE).

Guttman, L. (1944). A Basis for Scaling Qualitative Data. *American Sociological Review*, 9(2), 139–59.

Hagerty, M. R. (1999). Testing Maslow's Hierarchy of Needs: National Quality-of-Life across Time. *Social Indicators Research*, 46(3), 249–71.

Hayek, F. A. (1979). The Subjective Character of the Data of the Social Sciences. In F. A. Hayek (ed.), *The Counter-Revolution of Science: Studies on the Abuse of Reason*. Illinois: The Free Press Glencoe, pp. 25–35.

Hicks, N. and P. Streeten (1979). Indicators of Development: The Search for a Basic Needs Yardstick. *World Development*, 7, 567–80.

Hirsch, F. (1976). *Social Limits to Growth*. Cambridge, MA: Harvard University Press.

Houthakker, H. S. and L. D. Taylor (1970). *Consumer Demand in the United States: Analyses and Projections*. 2nd ed. Cambridge, MA: Harvard University Press.

Jackson, T. and N. Marks (1999). Consumption, Sustainable Welfare and Human needs – with Reference to UK Expenditure Patterns between 1954 and 1994. *Ecological Economics*, 28(3), 421–41.

Jevons, S. (1871; 1957). *The Theory of Political Economy.* New York: Sentry Press (Augustus M. Kelly reprints, 1965).

Katsulis, J. J., R. F. Lusch and E. F. Stafford Jr (1979). Consumer Acquisition Patterns for Durable Goods. *Journal of Consumer Research,* 6(1), 47–57.

Kay, P. (1964). A Guttman Scale Model of Tahitian Consumer Behavior. *Southwestern Journal of Anthropology,* 20(2), 160–7.

Keynes, J. M. (1933). *Essays in Persuasion.* New York: W. W. Norton.

Kobus, M. and Milos, P. (2012). Inequality Decomposition by Population Subgroups for Ordinal Data. *Journal of Health Economics,* 31, 15–21.

Kolm, S.-Ch. (1969). The Optimal Production of Social Justice. In H. Guitton & J. Margolis (eds.), *Public Economics,* London: Macmillan, pp. 145–200.

Lagueux, M. (1997). Menger and Jevons on Value: A Crucial Difference. Cahier No. 97-06, University of Montreal, Faculty of Arts and Sciences, Department of Philosophy. Montreal, Canada.

Lavoie, M. (1994). A Post Keynesian Approach to Consumer Choice. *Journal of Post Keynesian Economics,* 16(4), 539–62.

Lavoie, M. (2005). René Roy, the Separability and Subordination of Needs, and Post-Keynesian Consumer Theory. *History of Economics Review,* 42(1), 46–9.

Lazar, A., and J. Silber (2013). On the Cardinal Measurement of Health Inequality When Only Ordinal Information Is Available on Individual Health Status. *Health Economics,* 22, 106–13.

Leibenstein, H. (1950). Bandwagon, Snob, and Veblen Effects in the Theory of Consumer Demand. *Quarterly Journal of Economics,* 64, 183–207.

Little, I. M. D. (1950). The Theory of Consumer Behavior – A Comment. *Oxford Economic Papers,* 2, 132–5.

Lustig, N. and J. Silber (2016). Introduction to the Special Issue on Global Poverty Lines. *Journal of Economic Inequality,* 14(2), 129–40.

Lutz, M. A. and K. Lux (1979). *The Challenge of Humanistic Economics.* Menlo Park, CA: Benjamin/Cummings.

Lv, G., Y. Wang, and Y. Xu (2015). On a New Class of Measures for Health Inequality Based on Ordinal Data. *Journal of Economic Inequality,* 13(3), 465–77.

McFall, J. (1969). Priority Patterns and Consumer Behavior. *Journal of Marketing,* 33(4), 50–5.

Marshall, A. (1949). *Principles of Economics.* 8th ed., London: Macmillan.

Maslow, A. (1970). *Motivation and Personality.* New York: Harper and Row.

Max-Neef, M., A. Elizalde and M. Hopenhayn (1989). Human Scale Development: An Option for the Future. *Development Dialogue,* 1(1), 7–80.

Max-Neef, M. (1991). *Human Scale Development: Conception, Application, and Further Reflections*. New York and London: Apex Press.

Menger, C. (1871; 1981). *Principles of Economics*. New York: New York University Press.

Menger, C. (1923). *Grundsätze des Volkswirtschaftslehre. Zweite Auflage*. Wien, Leipzig: Hölder-Pichler-Tempsky A.G.

Neiman, B. and J. S. Vavra (2019). The Rise of Niche Consumption. Working paper No. 2019-102, The Becker-Friedman Institute at the University of Chicago.

Ngo, D. K. L. (2018). A Theory-Based Living Standards Index for Measuring Poverty in Developing Countries. *Journal of Development Economics*, 130, 190–202.

Pareto, V. (1895). La legge délia demanda. *Giornali degli economisti*, X, 59–68.

Paroush, J. (1963). The Order of Acquisition of Durable Goods. *Bank of Israel Survey* (in Hebrew), 2, 47–61.

Paroush, J. (1965). The Order of Acquisition of Consumer Durables. *Econometrica*, 33(1), 225–35.

Paroush, J. (1973). Efficient Purchasing Behavior and Order Relations in Consumption. *Kyklos*, XXVI (1), 91–112.

Pasinetti, L. L. (1981). *Structural Change and Economic Growth*. Cambridge: Cambridge University Press.

Plato (2007). *The Republic*. London: (Penguin Classics) Paperback, Penguin Random House.

Popper, K. (1959). *The Logic of Scientific Discovery*. Abingdon-on-Thames: Routledge.

Prais, S. J. (1952). Non-linear Estimates of the Engel Curve. *Review of Economic Studies*, 20(2), 87–104.

Raileanu Szeles, M. and A. Fusco (2013). Item Response Theory and the Measurement of Deprivation: Evidence from Luxembourg Data. *Quality and Quantity*, 47(3), 15–45.

Rasch, G. (1960). *Probabilistic Models for Some Intelligence and Attainment Tests*. Copenhagen: Danish Institute for Educational Research.

Reardon, S. F. (2009). Measures of Ordinal Segregation. *Research on Economic Inequality*, 17, 129–55.

Rippin, N. (2010). Poverty Severity in a Multidimensional Framework: The Issue of Inequality between Dimensions. Courant Research Center, Discussion Paper No. 47, University of Göttingen, Germany.

Rippin, N. (2012). Distributional Justice and Efficiency: Integrating Inequality within and between Dimensions in Additive Poverty Indices. Courant Research Centre – PEG, Discussion Papers 128, University of Göttingen, Germany.

Robinson, J. (1956). *The Accumulation of Capital*. London: Macmillan.

Roy, R. (1930). La Demande dans ses Rapports avec la Repartition des Revenus. *Metron*, VIII(3), 101–53.

Roy, R. (1931). Les Lois de la Demande. *Revue d'Economie Politique*, 45(4), 1190–218.

Roy, R. (1933). La Demande dans ses Rapports avec la Repartition des Revenus. *Econometrica*, 1(3), 265–73.

Roy, R. (1943). Hiérarchie des Besoins et la Notion de Groupes dans l'Economie de Choix. *Econometrica*, 11(1), 13–24.

Roy, R. (1947). La Distribution du Revenu Entre Les Divers Biens. *Econometrica*, 15(3), 205–25.

Ruprecht, W. (2007). From Carl Menger's Theory of Goods to an Evolutionary Approach to Consumer Behaviour. In M. Bianchi (ed.), *The Evolution of Consumption: Theories and Practices (Advances in Austrian Economics, Vol. 10)*, Bingley: Emerald Group, pp. 3–29.

Schultz, H. (1938). *The Theory and Measurement of Demand*. Chicago: University of Chicago Press.

Schwabe, H. (1868; 1966). *Das Verhältniss von Miethe und Einkommen in Berlin*. Ludwigshafen am Rhein: Hausbau Rheinland-Pfalz AG.

Sen, A. (1976). Poverty: An Ordinal Approach to Measurement. *Econometrica*, 44(2), 219–31.

Sen, A. (1980). Equality of What? Reprinted in A. Sen (1982), *Choice, Welfare and Measurement*, Oxford: Basic Blackwell.

Sen, A. (1983). Poor, Relatively Speaking. *Oxford Economic Papers*, 35(2), 153–69.

Silber, J. and G. Yalonetzky (2013). Measuring Multidimensional Deprivation with Dichotomized and Ordinal Variables. In G. Betti, and A. Lemmi (eds.), *Poverty and Social Exclusion: New Methods of Analysis, Routledge Advances in Social Economics*, New York: Routledge, pp. 9–37.

Simonin, J.-P. (2009). The Analysis of "Food Costs" by Jules Dupuit (1859) and René Roy's Hierarchy of Needs Theory (1943). *Revue Economique*, 60(6), 1455–67 (in French).

Smith, A. (1759; 1982). *The Theory of Moral Sentiments*. D. D. Raphael and A. L. Macfie (eds.), Indianapolis: Liberty Fund.

Smith, A. (1776; 1981). *An Inquiry into the Nature and Cause of the Wealth of Nations*. R. H. Campbell and A. S. Skinner (eds.), Indianapolis: Liberty Fund.

Soutar, G. N. and S. P. Cornish-Ward (1997). Ownership Patterns for Durable Goods and Financial Assets: A Rasch Analysis. *Applied Economics*, 29(7), 903–11.

Stafford Jr, E. F., J. J. Kasulis and R. L. Lusch (1982). Consumer Behavior in Accumulating Household Financial Assets. *Journal of Business Research*, 10, 397–417.

Stigler, G. J. (1954). The Early History of Empirical Studies of Consumer Behavior. *Journal of Political Economy*, 62(2), 95–113.

Streeten, P. (1984). Basic Needs: Some Unsettled Questions. *World Development*, 12(9), 973–8.

Theil, H. (1967). *Economics and Information Theory*. Amsterdam: North-Holland Publishing Company.

Veblen, T. (1931). *The Theory of the Leisure Class*. New York: Modern Library (originally published in 1899).

Witt, U. (2001). Learning to Consume – A Theory of Wants and the Growth of Demand. *Journal of Evolutionary Economics*, 11, 23–36.

Wolfson, M.C. (1994). When Inequalities Diverge. *American Economic Review*, 84(2), 353–58.

Working, H. (1943). Statistical Laws of Family Expenditure. *Journal of the American Statistical Association*, 38, 43–56.

Wright, C. D. (1875). *Sixth Annual Report of the Bureau of Labor Statistics*, Massachusetts Bureau of Statistics of Labor, Boston: Wright and Potter, p. 438.

Yalonetzky, G. (2012). Conditions for the Most Robust Multidimensional Poverty Comparisons Using Counting Measures and Ordinal Variables. ECINEQ Working Paper, 2012–257.

Yamamori, T. (2017). The Concept of Need in Adam Smith. *Cambridge Journal of Economics*, 41, 327–47.

Yamamori, T. (2018). The Concept of Need in Amartya Sen: Commentary to the Expanded Edition of Collective Choice and Social Welfare. *Ethics and Social Welfare*, 12(4), 387–92.

Yamamori, T. (2020). The Intersubjective Ontology of Need in Carl Menger. *Cambridge Journal of Economics*, 44, 1093–113.

Yalonetzky, G. (2012). Conditions for the Most Robust Multidimensional Poverty Comparisons Using Counting Measures and Ordinal Variables. ECINEQ Working Paper, 2012–257.

Zheng, B. (2011). A New Approach to Measure Socioeconomic Inequality in Health. *Journal of Economic Inequality*, 9(4), 555–77.

In honor of our colleague Jacob Paroush, who introduced us to the notion of order of acquisition of durable goods.

Cambridge Elements ≡

Development Economics

Series Editor-in-Chief

Kunal Sen
UNU-WIDER and University of Manchester

Kunal Sen, UNU-WIDER Director, is Editor-in-Chief of the Cambridge Elements in Development Economics series. Professor Sen has over three decades of experience in academic and applied development economics research, and has carried out extensive work on international finance, the political economy of inclusive growth, the dynamics of poverty, social exclusion, female labour force participation, and the informal sector in developing economies. His research has focused on India, East Asia, and sub-Saharan Africa.

In addition to his work as Professor of Development Economics at the University of Manchester, Kunal has been the Joint Research Director of the Effective States and Inclusive Development (ESID) Research Centre, and a Research Fellow at the Institute for Labor Economics (IZA). He has also served in advisory roles with national governments and bilateral and multilateral development agencies, including the UK's Department for International Development, Asian Development Bank, and the International Development Research Centre.

Thematic Editors

Tony Addison
University of Copenhagen, and UNU-WIDER

Tony Addison is a Professor of Economics in the University of Copenhagen's Development Economics Research Group. He is also a Non-Resident Senior Research Fellow at UNU-WIDER, Helsinki, where he was previously the Chief Economist-Deputy Director. In addition, he is Professor of Development Studies at the University of Manchester. His research interests focus on the extractive industries, energy transition, and macroeconomic policy for development.

Chris Barret
Johnson College of Business, Cornell University

Chris Barrett is an agricultural and development economist at Cornell University. He is the Stephen B. and Janice G. Ashley Professor of Applied Economics and Management; and International Professor of Agriculture at the Charles H. Dyson School of Applied Economics and Management. He is also an elected Fellow of the American Association for the Advancement of Science, the Agricultural and Applied Economics Association, and the African Association of Agricultural Economists.

Carlos Gradín
University of Vigo

Carlos Gradín is a professor of applied economics at the University of Vigo. His main research interest is the study of inequalities, with special attention to those that exist between population groups (e.g., by race or sex). His publications have contributed to improving the empirical evidence in developing and developed countries, as well as globally, and to improving the available data and methods used.

Rachel M. Gisselquist

UNU-WIDER

Rachel M. Gisselquist is a Senior Research Fellow and member of the Senior Management Team of UNU-WIDER. She specializes in the comparative politics of developing countries, with particular attention to issues of inequality, ethnic and identity politics, foreign aid and state building, democracy and governance, and sub-Saharan African politics. Dr Gisselquist has edited a dozen collections in these areas, and her articles are published in a range of leading journals.

Shareen Joshi

Georgetown University

Shareen Joshi is an Associate Professor of International Development at Georgetown University's School of Foreign Service in the United States. Her research focuses on issues of inequality, human capital investment and grassroots collective action in South Asia. Her work has been published in the fields of development economics, population studies, environmental studies and gender studies.

Patricia Justino

UNU-WIDER and IDS – UK

Patricia Justino is a Senior Research Fellow at UNU-WIDER and Professorial Fellow at the Institute of Development Studies (IDS) (on leave). Her research focuses on the relationship between political violence, governance and development outcomes. She has published widely in the fields of development economics and political economy and is the co-founder and co-director of the Households in Conflict Network (HiCN).

Marinella Leone

University of Pavia

Marinella Leone is an assistant professor at the Department of Economics and Management, University of Pavia, Italy. She is an applied development economist. Her more recent research focuses on the study of early child development parenting programmes, on education, and gender-based violence. In previous research she investigated the short-, long-term and intergenerational impact of conflicts on health, education and domestic violence. She has published in top journals in economics and development economics.

Jukka Pirttilä

University of Helsinki, and UNU-WIDER

Jukka Pirttilä is Professor of Public Economics at the University of Helsinki and VATT Institute for Economic Research. He is also a Non-Resident Senior Research Fellow at UNU-WIDER. His research focuses on tax policy, especially for developing countries. He is a co-principal investigator at the Finnish Centre of Excellence in Tax Systems Research.

Andy Sumner

King's College London, and UNU-WIDER

Andy Sumner is Professor of International Development at King's College London; a Non-Resident Senior Fellow at UNU-WIDER and a Fellow of the Academy of Social Sciences. He has published extensively in the areas of poverty, inequality, and economic development.

About the Series

Cambridge Elements in Development Economics is led by UNU-WIDER in partnership with Cambridge University Press. The series publishes authoritative studies on important topics in the field covering both micro and macro aspects of development economics.

United Nations University World Institute for Development Economics Research

United Nations University World Institute for Development Economics Research (UNU-WIDER) provides economic analysis and policy advice aiming to promote sustainable and equitable development for all. The institute began operations in 1985 in Helsinki, Finland, as the first research centre of the United Nations University. Today, it is one of the world's leading development economics think tanks, working closely with a vast network of academic researchers and policy makers, mostly based in the Global South.

Cambridge Elements ☰

Development Economics

Elements in the Series

A full series listing is available at: www.cambridge.org/CEDE

Printed in the United States
by Baker & Taylor Publisher Services